CANDID MUSINGS and PRACTICAL PARABLES

REV. FRED O. RICE

Copyright © 1998 by Evelyn Rice
All Rights Reserved
Printed by Wesley Press, Indianapolis, Indiana
United States of America
ISBN 0-89827-194-0

All rights reserved. No part of this publication may be reproduced, stored in a retrieval system, or transmitted in any form or by any means — electronic, mechanical, photocopy, recording or any other — except for brief quotations in printed reviews, without the prior written permission of Evelyn Rice, wife of the late Rev. Fred O. Rice.

TABLE OF CONTENTS

Acknowledgements 5
Poems 7
   Poems 9
   The Would-Be Poet 10
Church 11
   Ordination 13
   A Daffy Dinner 15
   A Tribute To Our Babies 16
   Christ's Ambassadors 17
   Easter Past 18
   Mothers and Daughters 19
   Old Evangel Days 20
   Sermonette 22
   The Race Is On 24
   The Sower 26
Friends 27
   Merry Christmas to the Procks 29
   Gilda Ruth Marion 30
   Retirement 32
   A Silver Wedding Tribute for Vester and Gilda Marion .. 33
   Sixty Years of Love 35
   The Big Six — Ohhhhhhh 38
Prayer & Praise 41
   A Prayer From Childhood 43
   A Prayer of Thanks 45
   A Sacrifice of Praise 46
   A Word of Thanks 47
   Now We See Thru A Glass Darkly 48
   "He Maketh Me to Lie Down" 49
   I Give You Thanks 50
   I'd Rather Preach 51
   The Master's Will 52
   Ready 53
   When You Don't Know What to Say—Say "Thank You, Lord" 54
   The Handicapped 55
Special Occasions 57
   From "Father's Side" 59
   "His Name" 61
   "If Jesus Had Not Come" 62
   It's Christmas Time Again 64
   Reflections 65
   The New Year 66
Potpourri 67
   The Tuner's Life 69
   A Diamond in the Rough 71
   Growing Old 72
   Hunting 74

My Potty-Chair. 75
Spring In Indiana 77
The Beast 78
The Dentist. 80
The Gloves. 83
The Saga of a Cadillac 84
To Lose or Not to Lose. 87

Family 89
A Small Surprise 91
Amber 92
Amber's Breakfast 93
Amber's Toys 94
A Boy's Tribute to Mother 95
Christmas Coming Late 96
Christmas Eve 98
Dear Mo. 100
Forty Years of Happiness 101
Friday Work 103
Happy Anniversary Dear. 104
Keep Faith 105
Life Ain't Fair 106
Memories of Dad 107
Mom's Ninety Years (Cronkhite) 108
A Mother's Day Tribute 111
Mother 113
My Dearly Beloved 115
My Sis 116
My New Year's Resolution 1974. 118
One Size Fits All. 119
Retirement 120
Sick and Tired 122
Sleep On. 123
Sleeping Beauty 124
Slim and Trim. 125
Spring and You. 126
Summer's Slipping By 127
The Gift 129
The Morn After Christmas 130
The Treasure Hunt 131
Those Golden Years 133
Thoughts of Mother 135
Three Days Till Christmas 137
To Go or Not to Go 139
To My Sleeping Beauty 141
My Tribute to Dad (Cronkhite) 142
To My Sweetheart 144
Weekend With Two Granddaughters 145
Work Day 148
Workday 150
The Rice Reunion 151

Tribute 153
A Tribute to my Dad. 155
Memories of Dad 157

Family Album 159

ACKNOWLEDGEMENTS

❧ A very special Thank You to Cheryl Rice (daughter-in-law) for the many, many hours it took to decipher Fred's writings that were written mostly on napkins and scrap paper and then placed in the computer so this book of poems could be possible.

❧ A very special Thank You to Debra Levite (niece-in-law) who volunteered her time typing, editing and managing this project.

❧ Thank you to my boys, Levi and Fred, Jr., for their concern and help to me during these days without Fred and for their loving tributes about their dad.

❧ Thank you to Betty Malz for assisting with the title of this book. Betty has been a good friend of the family for several years and I appreciate her help.

❧ Thank you to my God, for loving me and caring for me and providing His grace that is sufficient for all my needs.

Frances Evelyn Rice

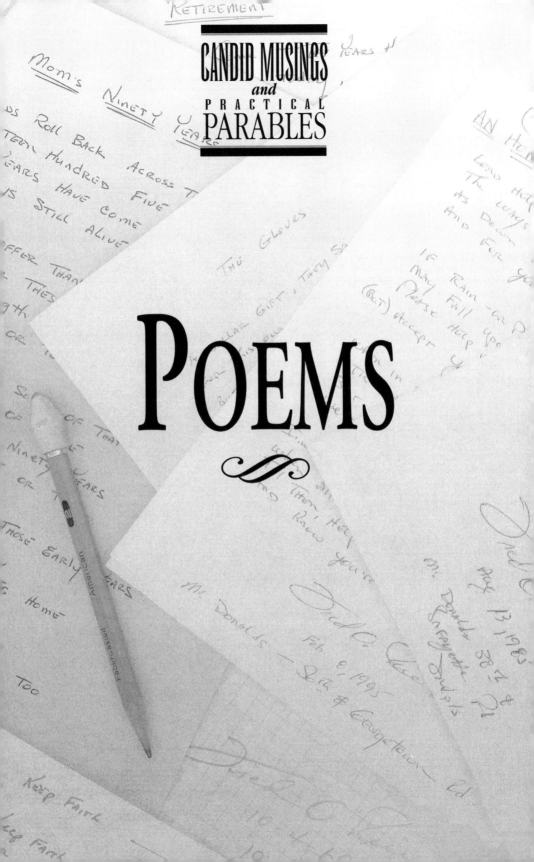

POEMS

A poem I've been asked to write,
For friends from time to time.
Seems folks do like the story told,
When it's been put in rhyme.

I started writing as a lad,
Didn't always turn out good.
But I still tried to write it down,
And did the best I could.

When but sixteen I tried to write,
About a move I made;
Fort Wayne the town, lived all alone,
The details from me fade.

That poem somehow lost with time,
Did probably not complete.
For just a kid I guess the job
Was just too big a feat.

I didn't give up—I still would try,
Then came a time to me.
By now I was a preaching kid,
Evangelist tried to be.

I wrote about my meetings and
I wrote about the way
When I would meet my wife to be,
A very special day.

As years they passed, I'd write a line,
My sermon to augment.
Or write about some special day
I'd with the family spent.

I wrote to Mom on Mother's Day,
Or wife on wedding day.
I'd try to put what felt inside,
And say a different way.

Though still I'm not a poet great,
I've satisfaction felt.
I won a trip to Gatlinburg,
As prizes out were dealt.

Been asked to write 'bout special friends,
For special kids of days.
Expressed for them just what they need,
Say what they want to say.

Someday I hope to dig them out,
These poems from the past.
And get them put into a book,
So they through years will last.

But if I do or if I don't,
I guess I'll always write;
To tell about the many things
That always are in sight.

8/22/85
Breakfast at Jo-Jo S. Lynhurst

THE WOULD-BE POET

I'm not a poet, Bard or Sage,
But often wish I were.
Because I love to write and tell,
When in or out somewhere.

I'd write about the little things,
We often overlook.
Or blessing that might come
  our way,
Or things that are from us took.

I'd write about the funny things,
Or things that are often sad.
I'd write about the good things
  too,
Sometimes the things that are
  bad.

I'd like to write 'bout people too,
And places where I've been.
Just tell in rhyme of all the fun,
And all the things I've seen.

Yes, I would tell of family too,
Of all my folk and kin.
Relate the stories they have
  shared,
Just flowing from my pen.

But since I'm not a poet nor
A writer, Bard nor Sage,
I'll never share what's deep
  inside,
To you on printed page.

Perhaps even yet in days to
  come,
I'll still a writer be.
Then all my friends and family
  too,
Can see inside of me.

August 13, 1985
McDonald's 38th and Lafayette Road,
Indianapolis

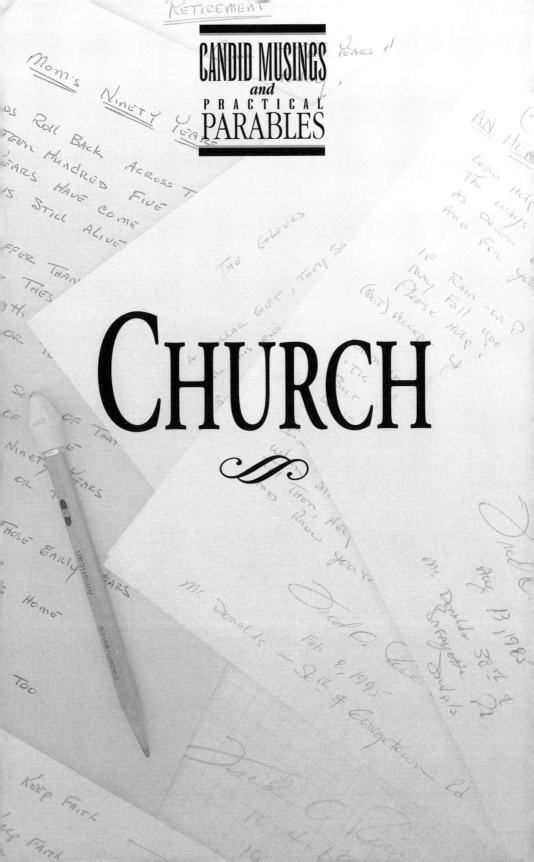

CANDID MUSINGS and PRACTICAL PARABLES

CHURCH

ORDINATION

"Ordination, what is that?"
Some folks may ask us.
"It can't be much," I hear them
    say,
"Why make this awful fuss?"

And true to some, it doesn't
    mean much,
Because they do not know.
God's plan for man, to take the
    Word,
And with its message go.

Please let me tell you what's
    involved,
To work and make the grade.
So one might hear that charge,
    "GO PREACH,
On you the task is laid."

It takes OMISSION of some
    things,
That one might hold quite near.
For Jesus said to leave behind,
Your house and loved ones dear.

And next a READINESS of
    heart,
To hear that voice so still.
That whispers, "come this way
    my son,
If you would know my will."

Then comes DESIRE for things
    of God,
Earth's pleasures cannot charm.
A separated life to lead,
Lest he should come to harm.

INSTRUCTION too must be a
    part,
Of this long winding trail.
God's Word to know, and others
    show,
In this he dare not fail.

He must be NOBLE in some
    ways,
Yet neither proud nor vain.
For he must reach both high and
    low,
And stand with those in pain.

It's now just half of this big
    word,
That we've initialized.
As you can see, it takes much
    more,
Than one might realize.

It takes AMBITION too, you
    know,
And TRIALS sure to be.
INVESTIGATIONS oft times
    come,
To ordination see.

The years they pass, but oh so slow,
He cries, "What's needed more?"
And then he sees some other things,
That are to come before.

OBEDIENCE to God and man,
The Church and District too.
Obey the bylaws, to be sure,
The Bible, Old and New.

Then finally after years of work,
Of preaching, prayers and tears.
"I'm NOTHING Lord," this young man cries,
"Please banish all my fears."

From voice so sweet he hears these words,
"You're ready now, my son,
"To be ordained and take my Word,
Choice servant you've become."

He stands at last with other men,
In ordination class.
Their wives close by, with great delight,
Their "preacher's" hand they clasp.

Commission given from The Book,
"I CHARGE YOU...PREACH THE WORD."
It seems to them the sweetest words,
That they have ever heard.

The joy that floods this young man's heart,
In words cannot be set.
For deep within he has a peace;
Provisions he has met.

He travels home with feelings mixed,
He's walking ten feet tall.
Yet humbled deeply with God's Grace,
For such an honored call.

ORDAINED...A preacher of God's Word,

ORDAINED...Christ's love to show.

ORDAINED...To follow where he leads,

ORDAINED...ORDAINED... TO GO!

Mark 16:15
"Go ye into all the world and preach the Gospel to every creature."
10/10/74

A DAFFY DINNER

A Daffy Dinner someone said,
I came around to see.
They're all just crazy in their head,
It seems like that to me.

Spaghetti served without a fork,
Just use a pick or straw.
While others sit around and laugh,
He-Haw—He-Haw—He-Haw.

You drink your ice cream, Jell-O too,
Your corn and beans come next.
Just how to eat them is your guess,
It seems you're in a fix.

The entertainment's something else,
The singers were a blast.
That make-up skit and elephant,
They also were a gas.

Now if we sleep at all tonight,
'Twill be a big surprise.
We'll all just toss and roll around,
Until it's time to rise.

I'm not too sure I'll try again,
A dinner just like this.
I think I'll find some good excuse,
So I will have to miss.

Pastor Rice
4-14-77

A Tribute To Our Babies

Our baby boys and baby girls,
'Bout the sweetest things on earth.
They find their place in heart
    and home,
From the moment of their birth.

That delicate flesh, those tiny hands,
And pretty little feet.
Those soft sweet eyes and tender
    cry,
Just makes a home complete.

It's all too quick, the days slip by,
And baby days are past,
Those little hands and little feet,
Have grown up far too fast.

Now for our babies of the church,
We're proud as we can be,
We'd like to show them off today,
So everyone can see.

It's Scripture to exalt a child,
Our Lord did it one day.
He set a child before the crowd,
And then explained the way.

"Like little children," Jesus said,
"Our lives must come to be,
If heaven's beauty, up above,
We ever hope to see."

We honor every baby here,
We pray God's blessings rest,
On every step of life ahead,
And trust each day be blest.

A special honor is bestowed,
A "baby of the year,"
It's little DAX, a special one,
He's everybody's dear.

We thought we'd lose him, at
    the first,
There were some anxious days.
But prayer was made, with trust
    above,
For healing, give God praise.

And since that time, our DAX
    was here,
Attendance record good.
His parents teaching him the way,
As Godly parents should.

So here we give our tribute to,
All babies here today,
May God now bless them
    through the years,
For this, we ever pray.

3-10-77

CHRIST'S AMBASSADORS

From the Pastor's Desk:

Christian Greetings!

As the Pastor of a wonderful C.A. group, I offer the following poem in their honor.

C.A.'S THE NAME
THEY PROUDLY WEAR,
AS JESUS' CROSS
THEY HUMBLY BEAR.
THIS BURDEN THEY
MOST GLADLY SHARE,

THEY'RE CHRIST'S
AMBASSADORS!

FOR LOST MANKIND
THEY SHOW THEY CARE,
THO' WAY BE ROUGH,
OR WEATHER FAIR,
SOUL SINKING DOWN,
TO SAVE...THEY DARE,

THEY'RE CHRIST'S
AMBASSADORS!

FROM PLEASURE VAIN,
APART THEY TEAR,
AS EARTHLY FRIENDS
IN WONDER STARE,
YES, THIS IS
DEDICATION RARE,

BUT, THEY'RE CHRIST'S
AMBASSADORS!

2 Corinthians 5:20

EASTER PAST

Easter Day has come and gone,
The message lingers still;
Of Christ our resurrected Lord,
Its joy my heart doth fill.

There's not a doubt of this bright hope,
Within my heart and mind;
But rather peace—assurance full,
In this report I find.

Because Christ lives—God's Word has said,
I too shall live for aye.
I'll go and dwell in heaven above,
Come Resurrection Day!

(Wednesday Past Easter)
April 11, 1992
Hardee's Castleton

Mothers and Daughters

Mothers, Daughters, here tonight,
Faces shining oh so bright.
Giving out a radiant light,
Seems to me a lovely sight.

Speaks of love betwixt the two,
Old relation, ever new.
Things together they will do,
Love they say, I have for you.

Makes each home a happy place,
Looking at each other's face.
Better than all silk and lace,
This reflects a heavenly grace.

"Mother dear," the daughter's say,
"All my life you make so gay.
Live forever, this I pray,
God grant strength from day
   to day."

"Daughter mine, you are so dear,"
These sweet words from moms
   I hear.
"Your young life I hope to steer,
From God's path, you'll never
   veer."

As we look about right now,
Mothers...Daughters, humbly
   bow.
Pray to God, His grace endow,
Place His hand upon each brow.

Work together hand in hand,
With our family we will stand.
'gainst all problems we will
   band,
Long as we live in this land.

P.S. Mothers, Daughters, fight
   some too,
This bold fact is not too new.
E'en though disagreements
   brew,
Hours of anger are quite few.

4-30-76

OLD EVANGEL DAYS

We've come today
To reminisce,
An era passed away.
For me it's
Twenty years and more,
Just seems like yesterday.

I came with family,
Wife and boys,
New pastors, were to be.
A little church,
The near west side,
Not really much to see.

We felt God's will
To make the move,
Though didn't understand.
Just what would be
In days ahead,
Or what would be God's plan.

The church was cute,
The carpet red,
Remodeled, one could see.
The crowd was small,
But folks were kind,
To wife, my boys and me.

Remember well,
Some faces bright,
Who've now passed on ahead.
We'll meet them all
When Jesus comes,
They'll rise up from the dead.

There's
UNCLE CHARLIE
    DAVENPORT,
And sweet AUNT LULU CREED.
See LUCILLE FARLEY,
With her smile,
ED CAGLE...yes indeed.

Then sister HALLIE ABRAHAM,
Oh yes...FRED ROBERTSON,
With SISTER BESSIE
Left behind,
Her task was not yet done.

Pop Buckner
Stands out in my mind,
Along with Mom he came.
And Sister Short,
Didn't show her age,
Was Ninety, just the same.

I think of DENNIS
With the kids,
A twinkle in his eyes.
He, too, has traveled
To that land,
Where there are no good-byes.

Remember some
Who moved away,
Belongings in their hand.
Like BILL & JANET
GEORGE & JEAN,
Bound for "The Promised
   Land"(Kentucky).

With many others,
There that day,
Each sitting in their place,
I'm sorry I
Can't name them all
In this allotted space.

Those early days,
I well recall,
The people had one mind.
To build a church,
Resources low....
A building lot must find.

No bed of ease,
We saw rough days,
Faith...skills...and patience tried.
But thank the Lord,
The church was built,
For God was on our side.

The years that followed,
God did bless,
New families came our way.
As testimony of
God's grace and love,
The church...it stands today!

This group that shared
Each others lives,
Have moved about through time.
But there's a bond,
That still unites,
Each heart with that of mine.

A bond of LOVE,
Still binds our hearts,
Across the miles and years.
We often share
Each others joys,
And share each other's tears.

I wish to share
The love I feel,
By varied means and ways.
I'm proud to be
A little part
Of OLD EVANGEL DAYS!

Former Pastor
October 1966 - February 1978

Written Sept. 14, 1988
for the Evangel picnic to be 9/17/88
at the request of Ralph Leviska

SERMONETTE

A preacher I confess I'm not,
Though I've been asked to share.
A sermonette with you tonight,
I don't think it's quite fair.

But I will try and add my part,
I'll tell of moms and girls.
Who had a place in history,
And some were really pearls.

We'll start with Moses' mother and,
His sister Miriam too.
Who worked together for a cause,
God's will they surely knew.

The ark was hid by Jocabed,
Among the river weeds.
And watched by sister, Miriam,
To see the baby's needs.

The teamwork of that mom
   and gal,
Should shame all Israel's men.
Brought death to Pharaoh and
   his force,
Exposed them of their sin.

Then next of Naaman's maid
   we read,
Her face shone with a gleam.
Spoke words of healing to her
   Lord,
A girl of just sixteen.

That girl's not heard of anymore,
In Bible history.
But I feel sure she has a place,
In heaven her face we'll see.

In Judges, too, we read about,
A soldier's daughter brave.
Who gave her life to pay a vow,
Her father's honor save.

Yes, such devotion's hard to find,
In this old world today.
But it's rewarded by our Lord,
God's words so plainly say.

The Bible speaks of others, too,
Some older girls who gave
Their lives to God with great
   delight,
And storms of life they'd brave.

Remember Martha? One who
   served,
Our Lord a lovely meal.
While others came to bring
   their sick,
For the Son of God to heal.

Then Mary who sat at His feet,
His blessed words to hear.
They calmed the tempest of
   her life,
And drove away her fear.

Now last, not least, by any means,
One more I'd like to give.
A girl who stands above the rest,
The purest life did live.

She far outshines the other girls,
No other in the land
Would thus be honored by the Lord,
Nor thus would feel His hand.

Her name was Mary, this you knew,
The mother of our King.
The night she brought Him to this world,
It made the angels sing.

Now just give thought to what would be,
If girls didn't do their part.
Of work undone, and souls lost too,
Would break the Savior's heart.

Yes, there's a place for girls today,
A place for mothers, too.
A place for all who love the Lord,
A place for me and you !

4-30-76

THE RACE IS ON
Hebrews 12:1

THE RACE IS ON...to spread God's Word,
Ere setting of the sun.
The fields are white, the harvest ripe,
The lost they must be won.

THE RACE IS ON...against the foe,
He too is running strong.
So we must run, be wary not,
Though days be hard and long.

THE RACE IS ON..."Light For The Lost,"
Who've never been informed
Of God's great love, to all mankind,
Nor of the judgment warned.

THE RACE IS ON...what's our reply,
When we in judgment stand.
If here we've failed to run our best,
No sheaves hold in our hand?

THE RACE IS ON...we must arise,
Must lay aside each weight.
Must run with patience to the end,
Where victors crowns await.

THE RACE IS ON...we'll "Send The Light,"
To souls in dark despair.
Much faster than we've run before,
Our Savior's love to share.

Lost souls beyond, in dark despair,
The shades of night draw near.
THE RACE IS ON to speed God's Word,
Should they the gospel hear.

We hear their cry from foreign lands,
Men groping for the light.
The task is clear, they must be taught,
And shown which way is right.

A race to run, against great odds,
Must run without delay.
To bring good news of Jesus' love,
And point lost men the way.

What answer then, on judgment day,
If we've not faithful been?
No sheaves to hold before our Lord,
And no reward to win.

"Say not four months"...the master said,
"The fields are white today."
"The harvest ripe"...it must be saved,
Run now without delay.

THE RACE IS ON.....our mission clear,
His light the world around.
We'll run the race, and faithful be,
Until the trumpet sound!

2-6-85
Written for Wanda Prock
for Light For The Lost Convention

THE SOWER

A farmer went to plant one day,
Good seed he had in hand.
He spread it out where 'ere he walked,
Yes, all across the land.

Some seed it fell upon the rocks,
It sprang up much too soon.
Because it had no root or rain,
Was scorched before 'twas noon.

Some seed it fell among the thorns,
Was choked and soon was dead.
No grain to come upon this wheat,
No lovely golden head.

But some seed fell upon good ground,
Sprang forth the harvest grain.
Some 30—60—hundred fold,
Mid softly falling rain.

What meaneth this, the question asked,
By those who heard this tale.
The Master said I'll tell just you,
So you will never fail.

The seed's God's Word, the field the world,
God's Word you each must sow.
As multitudes around you see,
Into them you must go.

Not all will hear the Word you speak,
The Devil all around.
To steal the seed and rob the mass,
As you strive to abound.

The thorns denote the cares of life,
And riches man does seek.
They choke the grain from growing up,
New converts are too weak.

But some seed grows to harvest full,
It brings forth as it should.
Your work rewarded after all,
As Jesus said it would.

Lord help me be as sower true,
To spread God's precious seeds.
To see a harvest from my work,
And help to meet man's need.

6-8-83
Bloomington, IN McDonald's

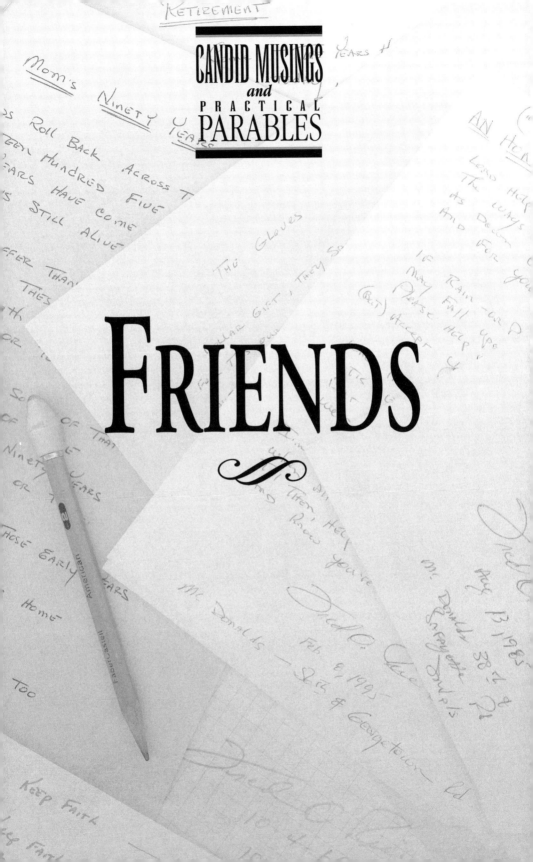

CANDID MUSINGS and PRACTICAL PARABLES

FRIENDS

MERRY CHRISTMAS TO THE PROCKS

To have a friend like you means more,
Than words could ere express.
Your very "friendship" means so much,
We stand expressionless.

What's there to give to friends today,
We have most everything.
Yet at this time of year we feel,
A gift we'd like to bring.

We've thought of tools....toys for the kids,
Or clothes for mom and dad.
But we don't know what size or shape,
Our choice....it might be bad.

Yet for our friends whose name is "PROCK,"
Some gift we'd like to share.
To show our love to folks like you,
And let you know we care.

Enclosed you'll find some tickets for,
A sport you might enjoy.
A "Tractor Pull"...we think you'll like,
Since you're an old "Farm Boy."

We'll pick you up in plenty of time,
And take you out with us.
We hope you'll like this little gift,
Now have a nice Christmas!

From
"THE RICES"
With Love

"1975"

Gilda Ruth Marion
Mystery Mother 1976

Our Mystery Mother for the year,
We honor her today.
A mother special to the church,
I'm sure you all will say.

She's not too young, yet not too old,
A family just 'bout right.
Three girls, one boy and husband too,
And grandkids her delight.

Some reasons why we've chosen her,
We'd like to share with you.
"Twill please you all to share with us,
Her virtues not a few.

First let us speak of "faithfulness"
Dates back for many years.
She's stood the test of time you see,
Through sorrows, joys and fears.

Each Sunday she is always here,
If it's within her might.
On Wednesday, too, just look around,
She's sure to be in sight.

She's been most faithful to the church
And worked wherever asked.,
In Nursery Class or WMC
Been faithful to her task.

She never needs that extra "thanks"
Or visit from the board,
To keep her faithful in her place;
She's working for the Lord.

Another virtue most to note,
Is that of "Attitude."
She's unassuming, kind and true,
You'll never see her rude.

We've seen the times when life's cruel way,
Has caused her pain and grief.
But we've observed her faith in God,
That brought her sweet relief.

Her girls have watched their
  mother's life,
And followed in her way.
They too are faithful in the
  church,
They're with her here today.

Yes, "GILDA RUTH," this is
  your day,
With family gathered near.
We join with them this Mother's
  Day,
To say, "WE THINK YOU'RE
  DEAR."

5-8-76

Read by Frances E. Rice
Mother's Day May 9, 1976
First Assembly of God
Speedway, Indiana

RETIREMENT

A day we all look forward to,
That seems will never come.
But years do pass, though sometimes slow,
This day, it reaches some.

It comes to many with their age,
Oft-times for service past.
And when it dawns, which e'er the case,
May it forever last.

We honor one who's reached that day,
Has worked her share and more.
She's faithful been, can lay it down,
Won't have to work any more.

"Retirement Day" I'm speaking of,
This day of joy we share.
As she shall leave her job behind,
Without a fret or care.

Awake when e'er she chooses to,
Get up…or lay in bed.
Eat breakfast late, then sit around,
Until the paper's read.

Perhaps she'll have more time to shop,
And spend some of that "green."
Or travel where she has not gone,
See sights she's never seen.

Or maybe she'll just pester Ray,
An errand, job or chore.
Just keep him busy—this and that,
Or drive her to the store.

Now EDITH, Here's our wish to you,
"THE BEST EACH COMING YEAR."
And as you live the life of ease,
PLEASE…think of us back here!

P.S. "Our day will come"

By Fred O. Rice, Sr. (Nov. 30, 1985)
In honor of EDITH PEARSON
upon her retirement

A Silver Wedding Tribute For Vesper and Gilda Marion 1952-1977

Our minds reflect across the years,
This special wedding day.
A sacred memory celebrate,
Of time now passed away.

The honored guests are here today,
With friends and family near.
We share their joy and happiness,
On this, their "Silver Year."

Let's take a look into the past,
Relive some bygone days.
We'll share some joys that came to them,
And learn some of their ways.

First Gilda Ruth, just "Sweet Sixteen"
...Perhaps a little more.
Had come to town to look for work,
So young and not too sure.

RED BOILING SPRINGS, in Tennessee,
The town she left behind.
A name like that you'd need to leave,
If work you hoped to find.

And Vesper too, had come to town,
From down Kentucky way.
Scottsville didn't offer future for
Young men, I heard them say.

continued

Both far from home in Indy town,
Their paths were deigned to cross.
They fell in love and quickly knew,
Their moves were not a loss.

Their courtship followed, this we know,
And plans all fell in place.
The date was set to say their vows,
They'd found each others grace.

September sixth, would be the day,
Year nineteen fifty-two.
They pledged their love and took an oath,
A promise to be true.

God blessed this couple, in due time,
As days they came and went.
For in their home, to bring it life,
A baby girl was sent.

They named her Kathy, then they said,
Some sisters for her play.
So God sent Nancy, first along,
Then Lisa too, that way.

Three girls, and yet is home complete,
Without a baby boy?
So here came Denny Wayne along,
To bring that extra joy.

Their home like most has happy been,
Yet not without its tears.
For sorrow and some clouds of life,
Has hovered through the years.

When storm clouds rose and problems came,
And dark would seem the night.
This family stood fast through the test,
Until the morning light.

A milestone we pass today,
A victory to be sure.
A couple true these many years,
And yet today are pure.

Our tribute now, we pay today,
The "MARIONS" we admire.
We pray God bless in future years,
And grant their heart's desire.

9-10-77

Sixty Years of Love
(Joseph Philip Malandro & Castelina Cateline)

The year was nineteen thirty-two,
October Twelve the day.
A couple stood and pledged their vows,
This love would last for aye.

A great depression in the land,
Not knowing what's ahead.
They built their home on love and trust,
Without a fear or dread.

Now "Joe" and "Custa" were the names,
This carefree, happy pair.
They clasped their hands in unison,
No worry, doubt or care.

Their honeymoon, a special treat
In those depression days.
Niagara Falls would be the place,
Plan future, means and ways.

God blessed this union, to be sure,
Two children came their way.
'Twas "Joe" and "Patty" from the Lord,
That brought such joy each day.

Now "Papa Joe", he worked so hard,
We're proud this day to say.
In all those years, yes, forty-one,
He never missed a day.

continued

His total years were forty-six,
Not only was he there,
But he was prompt, yes, never late,
This record is quite rare.

Now "Mama Custa" did her part,
Though she was in the house.
She cooked the meals and kept the home,
A faithful mother and spouse.

Italian Dishes, her forte',
For friends and family, too.
Have been remembered through the years,
By more than just a few.

Might mention here, if some don't know,
About our Mama Dear;
COUNTRY MUSIC was her "thing,"
Those songs she loved to hear.

She had a favorite country star,
"Big Slim The Lone Cowboy,"
And all his country western tunes
Brought her a lot of joy.

Now Dad, he had his weakness, too,
He loved his SPORTS quite well.
Those baseball games didn't want to miss,
We hear his family tell.

Would take his son and brothers too,
To see the Pirates play.
Would yell and scream—a true-blue fan,
When they the "Cards" would slay.

He also had a serious side,
And "music" made his day.
In church...at home...most anywhere,
Violin, he loved to play.

On Christmas Eve when all was still,
Some in his family said,
He'd get his violin out,
All others in their bed.

Then carols sweet would fill the air,
Sweet music it would ring.
And Christmas cheer would fill the home,
Such "Yuletide" joy 'twould bring.

The years slipped by, the kids grew up,
Their families now are grown.
And eight grand-children—plus six greats,
Have families of their own.

The folks didn't have the pleasure of
Their children being near.
Both Joe and Patty lived away
From Mom and Dad so dear.

To fill the gap the children left
When moving far from home,
The folks had their
    brothers...sister too,
Not leaving them alone.

We'd be remiss to not include,
About their Christian life.
This man knew Christ, his
    Savior-Lord,
As did his loving wife.

Their family now reflects the
    faith
That kept them through the
    years.
A Faith In God for EVERY
    need,
With smiles in tears.

Now SIXTY YEARS have come
    and gone
Since that young couple stood,
To pledge their love "forever"
IT LASTED—as it should.

It lasted when the days were
    dark,
In good times and in pain.
In happiness or sorrow deep,
In sunshine and in rain.

This love will keep on standing,
As in the days of yore.
God bless their years together,
And give them many more!

And now a prayer, for both
    of you,
"GOD WIPE AWAY ALL
    TEARS.
MAY YOU KNOW PEACE
    AND HAPPINESS,
IN ALL YOUR FUTURE
    YEARS."

To my very good friends, on your 60th Anniversary, BEST WISHES and GOD BLESS YOU!!

October 12, 1992

THE BIG SIX – OHHHHHHH

The year was nineteen-thirty three,
Missouri was the state.
The stork arrived, a gift to leave,
On his appointed date.

A baby boy with lots of joy,
That only sons can bring.
"The name is Roy," his folks announced,
Like music it did ring.

To tell of all the boyhood stuff
He did those early years.
We won't indulge in this short space,
Might only bring some tears.

The time flew by; yes, all too fast,
His teens and twenties too.
Yes, 30's, 40's, 50's, all,
Might wish it weren't true.

Now here we are, year '93,
Roy, maybe you should sit.
(for) The BIG "60" has come your way,
As older you did get.
No, really now, it's not so bad,
It's in the frame of mind.
For sixties bring some things to you,
That younger years can't find.

Your family's raised, that worry past,
Your days have less demand.
Can come and go with peace of mind,
Heed Wanda's each command.

Can hunt and fish, there's time for that,
See friends and family too.
Enjoy your kids, and grandkids more,
Do things you want to do.

Now as we come to think of it,
This "60" ain't so bad.
It's really what you've dreamed about,
Since you were just a lad.

So "HAPPY BIRTHDAY"
 to you, Roy,
Best wishes on your day.
Our prayers that God's
 continued love,
Be with you all life's way.

Your Friend,

P. S. It doesn't seem possible that I have known you and been your friend for almost half of those 60 years. It has been a good relationship which Frances and I have enjoyed and trust it continues until God calls all home.

GOD BLESS YOU ! !

(The Preacher)

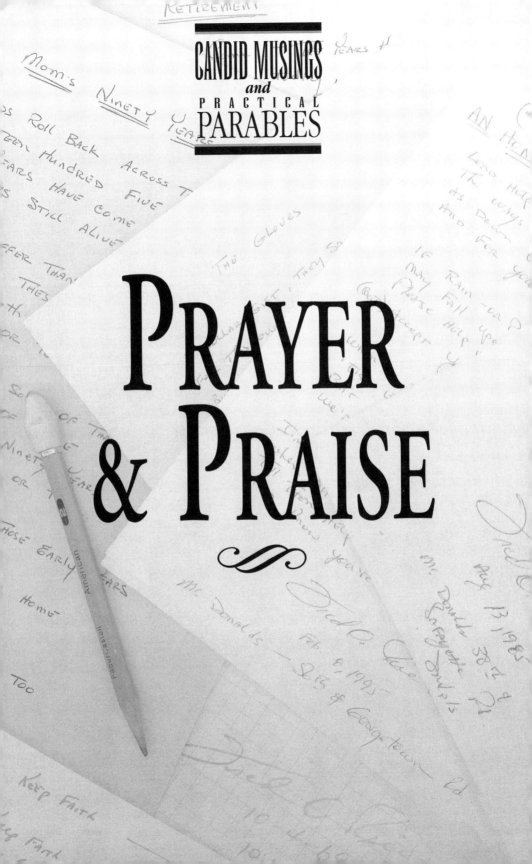

A Prayer From Childhood

"NOW I LAY ME DOWN TO SLEEP,"
That childhood prayer of yore,
I prayed again the other night,
'Twas more than just folklore.

"If I should die before I wake,"
So many times I've said,
And then I'd jump up from my knees,
And tumble into bed.

I'd near forgotten those childhood words
Until the other night,
As in intensive care I lay;
My future not so bright.

They had me wired to some machine,
IV's stuck in my arm.
My family sat in great suspense;
My church expressed alarm.

The nurses came all through the night,
My pulse was beating slow.
My pressure, too, they kept in check,
For it had dropped quite low.

A shot of morphine for the pain,
A pill for this or that.
While all the time just down the hall,
A worried family sat.

I watched my heartbeat on the scope,
Things falling now in place.
By then I knew it for a fact,
With death I'd run a race.

"If I should die before I wake,"
Those words rang loud and clear;
For now the first time in my life,
I knew that death was near.

How sweet the comfort from above,
To know that it would be,
"If I should die before I wake,"
My blessed Lord I'd see.

For seven days intensive care,
Eleven more outside.
Those eighteen days, emotions mixed,
My feelings hard to hide.

continued

The danger's past, I'm back at home,
Recovery's under way.
And with new meaning in those words,
My childhood prayer I pray.

"NOW I LAY ME DOWN TO SLEEP"
I say to God above.
"I PRAY THE LORD MY SOUL TO KEEP"
In His great arms of love.

"IF I SHOULD DIE BEFORE I WAKE"
I ask of God anew.
"I PRAY THE LORD MY SOUL TO TAKE"
To ever be with you.

4/10/76

A Prayer of Thanks

I pray my prayer again today,
As I have done before.
To just say "Thanks" my Lord to Thee,
It's what I feel—and more.

You've been so good from day to day,
Your blessings I have seen.
Of life and light, yes, joy & strength,
Your blood to wash me clean.

Now as I go upon my way,
With thanks upon my heart.
I pray your presence will abide,
And never from me part.

And I shall also lean on Thee,
Keep You upon my mind.
That I Your hand will always feel,
And perfect will I'll find.

P.S. I thank You for employment, too,
Supplying all my need.
As David said "I shall not want,"
In pastures green I'll feed.

I thank you Lord!!!

5/11/83
McDonald's
Bloomington, In

A Sacrifice of Praise

"I will bless the Lord at all
   times" (Psalm 34:1)
The Psalmist, he did say.
"His praise shall continually be
   in my mouth"
At night as well as day.

"In everything give thanks"
'Tis in His Holy Book.
In joy, or times of testing,
Regardless how things look.
   (1 Thess 5:18)

"This is the Will of God,
Concerning you," I read.
It lets me know He's watching
   o'er,
Will supply my every need.

Not always praise Him "for"
   the test,
Or trials that I face.
But praise Him "in" the trying
   times,
While running here life's race.

Praise Him in spite of need
   or woe,
Praise Him in spite of pain.
Praise Him because He still is
   God,
Praise Him to victory gain.

I'll praise you Lord, with all
   my heart,
I'll praise you night and day.
I'll praise you long as I have
   breath,
Till you call me away.

3-18-92
Hardees - 71st & I-465

A Word of Thanks

Dear Lord I wish
To give you thanks,
For all your loving care.
For all good things
You give to me,
Both common and things rare.

I thank you for
The health and strength,
The work you give to me.
The comforts of
This life each day,
That I am blessed to see.

Especially I give you thanks,
Next month will be twelve
    years.
Since I was stricken
In my heart,
Caused pain and fear and tears.

Those years have passed
Without great stress,
My problems have been few.
My heart has worked
And I am well,
All thanks I give to You.

You've not seen fit
To heal complete;
My strength's from day to day.
But that is all
I must expect,
"Each Day" the Scriptures say.

I give to you a special thanks,
For just some weeks ago,
I thought my heart
Had given out,
My pulse was beating slow.

But thanks to God
He heard my cry,
I'm up to strength today.
I'll give Him thanks
With all my heart,
Both now and yet for aye.

Hardees
Danville
2-26-88

Now We See Thru a Glass Darkly
An Honest Prayer

Lord help me not to question,
The ways that you do lead.
As down life's path I travel,
And for your help oft plead.

If rain or pain or sorrow,
May fall upon my way.
Please help me ne'er to grumble,
(But) accept your will each day.

When in the days of blessing,
'Tis easy to be glad.
But mid dark clouds of testing,
We're tempted to be sad.

I'm sure the day is coming,
When all will be made clear;
Till then, help me to trust, Lord,
And know you're always near!

Feb. 8, 1995
McDonalds - 56th and Georgetown Rd.

"He Maketh Me to Lie Down"

"Lie down," I hear my Shepherd
    say,
"The path is rough and steep."
But in my selfish headlong way,
His words I do not keep.

Oh foolish man who thinks to
    know,
More than his Shepherd dear,
Goes on his way and fails to heed,
God's voice he will not hear.

Then comes that sharp yet sweet
    command,
"Lie down, I say to thee,"
And with His firm, but gentle
    hand,
He stops me...tenderly.

Unpleasant are those days, for
    sure,
When we must quiet be,
But in that time of still recluse,
He gently talks to me.

He speaks, I listen, then I think,
What have my motives been?
Have I been working for the Lord,
Or to be seen of men?
The past, the future, present too,
All flow before my mind.
I pray, "Oh God, help me to
    know,
Thy will help me to find."

"Lie down," again I hear him
    say,
"Thy strength indeed is small.
In thy weakness watch and pray,
In Me thine all in all."

Then when the time has come
    and gone,
New strength's mine from
    above.
With joy I'll look upon those
    days,
And thank God for His love.

Because, "HE MAKETH ME TO LIE DOWN!"
(Psalm 23:2)

Inspired by my sister
Odessa Contat in her 4-7-76
visit to me 4-4-76 Westview Hospital
Indianapolis, Ind.

I Give You Thanks

My Father God, I give Thee
   thanks,
For answered prayer—and more.
For things I've asked from day
   to day,
And days gone on before.

I'm thinking most of what I
   prayed,
In February past.
Through March and April,
   burdened still,
My problem seemed so vast.

You heard my prayer before I
   prayed,
You knew the cry I'd make.
You sent a dream some days
   ahead,
A storm, and then a snake.

I knew not then, just what they
   were,
Nor why the dreams were sent.
Yet felt for sure a message
   come,
But knew not what it meant.

It wasn't long till storm clouds
   came,
(And) the serpent reared at me.
I asked myself was this my
   dream?
I'd have to wait and see.

I prayed to God to let it be,
As in the dreams had been.
The storm it never really hit,
I'd o'er the serpent win.

The clouds have passed—the
   serpent fled,
Dear God I give You thanks.
I'm glad I'm in Your army, Lord,
A soldier in Your ranks.

Accept my thanks again today,
I pray it from my heart.
Let me keep on and do Your
   will,
And never from You part.

5-9-83
McDonald's, Carmel, Ind.

I'D RATHER PREACH

I'm thankful Lord
You know my heart,
For all You've given me.

But deep inside
There is a void,
That no one else can see.

You've given work
A living good,
I surely can't complain.

But mid it all
That empty spot,
Brings sorrow and some pain.

Since just a child
My deep desire,
Has been to preach God's Word.

For thirty years
Since just nineteen,
That longing You have heard.

You've granted me
My heart's desire,
Your favor I did find.

Revival meetings
Pastorate too,
You were so good and kind.

I can't explain
Just why it is,
That sickness came my way.

My nerves - my mind
A heart attack,
Just don't know what to say.

I left my church
I felt 'twas best,
For them - and yes, for me.

But still expected
Some to preach,
And speak His Word you see.

But when I try
My mind goes wild,
Emotions can't control.

Not like the past
When I was young,
And words would simply roll.

I do my work
From day to day,
I have no goal to reach.

It simply boils
Down to this,
Dear Lord I'd rather preach!

Hardees 5-31-88
A Sequel to the prior poem
"I'd Rather Preach"

THE MASTER'S WILL

I cannot say
With that complaint,
I know God's ways are best.
He has a plan
In every life,
It's mine to stand the test.

If in His will
The day should come,
A healing I enjoy.
'Twould thrill my heart
To once again,
Be back in His employ.

If in His will
He has other plans,
These latter years ahead.
Then I shall say
"Thy will be done,"
I'll have no fear or dread.

Remember how
The Scripture states,
The potter molds the clay.
The clay is subject
To His will,
The Master knows the way.

My prayer is this
Lord let me live,
In Your most perfect will.
To preach or not
Is in Your plan,
I wait, yielded and still.

June 11, 1988

READY

I face death's river unafraid,
For with faith's eye, I see.
My loving Savior standing there,
 (Acts 7:56)
To greet and welcome me.

Though now I see through
 darkened glass,
Some things He won't reveal.
 (1 Cor. 13:12)
He'll help me cross the
 Jordan dark,
And at His feet I'll kneel.

He'll say well done and
 welcome home,
Your race on earth is past.
 (Matt. 25:21)
Receive a crown, and stone of
 white, (2 Tim. 4:8)
The victory's yours at last.
 (Rev. 2:17)

Then after greeting Mom and Dad,
With others now above. Matt. 8:11
I'll humbly stand at Jesus' side,
And thank Him for His love.

The weakness of this earthly house,
Will be dissolved, I read.
 (2 Cor. 5:1)
And one that can't be made with
 hands,
Will meet my every need.

I'll have new strength, to Praise
 the Lord (Psa. 103:5)
The Lamb for sinners slain.
 (1 Cor. 15:54)
And while eternal ages roll,
I'll every promise claim.

Don't weep as those who have
 no hope, (1 Thess. 4:13)
I've entered into rest.
I've heard, "Well Done...you've
 won the race,
Now enter heaven's best."

Just keep your faith and never
 doubt,
For heaven's now in view.
He giveth grace through darkest
 night,
Especially, just for you.

The promise is, "He'll soon
 Return," (1Thess. 4:16)
And then we all shall meet
Our family circle, all in one,
Together at His feet.

Fred O. Rice, Sr. 6/29/77

When You Don't Know What to Say— Say "Thank You, Lord"

What should I write,
As here I sit,
Just killing time this day.
There's nothing new,
That one might say,
I'm neither sad nor gay.

I might give thanks
For sunshine bright,
Its beauty warms my heart.
As here I sit
Just biding time,
Before my day I start.

I give all thanks
To God above,
From whom that sunshine came.
But whether sun
Or cloudy skies,
I thank Him all the same.

How sad 'twould be
To only thank
Him for the blessings fair.
And then despise
This God of love,
When dark days we must share.

This prayer I pray
It's from my heart,
"Accept my thanks, dear God."
I love you now,
I'll love for aye,
All years I walk this sod.

February 23, 1984
Hardees
Castleton by Wilking

THE HANDICAPPED

I thank you, God,
For health and strength,
For a mind that's bright and clear.
Those things we take
For granted oft,
Forget those blessings dear.

I praise you, God,
This very hour,
Reminded, as I've seen.
A group retarded,
Walk a path
That I have never been.

Oft times I grumble
'Cause I'm slow
To grasp and think and speak.
Forgive me Lord
And help me find
Forgiveness, I will seek!!

God bless the people,
Those who care,
Who watch and tend these ones.
For though they can't
Care for themselves,
They're still God's chosen sons.

By contrast in
Another room,
A birthday party gay.
The children all with
Minds so bright,
Enjoy a special day.

I'm prone to question,
Why are some
Afflicted as these few?
I'll leave the answer
In God's great hands,
For He loves the helpless too!!

Thurs. 10-17-85
96th & Meridian
(A group of retarded people came into
McDonald's where I ate - my heart
went out to them.)

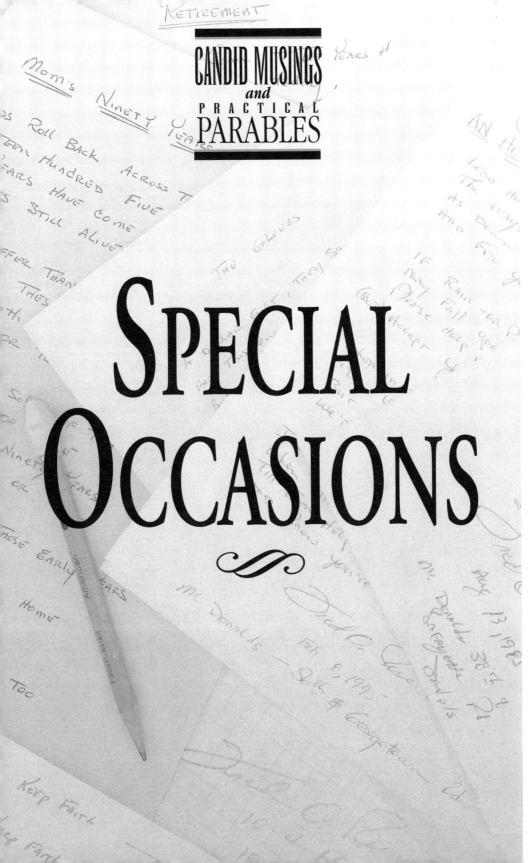

From "Father's Side"

The day to honor Dad has come,
This year like all the rest.
To some it's just another day,
To others, it's the best.

Our thoughts are different on
   this day,
For most it's joy and bliss.
While others think of dads
   gone on,
Their memories reminisce.

But a Dad, I'd like to show,
The picture from my side.
And share some feelings fathers
   have,
Though often try to hide.

As Father, I am proud to have,
A family round 'bout me.
They bring me joy beyond
   compare,
As others plainly see.

I'm thankful for a faithful wife,
On every Father's Day.
Who brought my children in
   the world,
"They're the smartest kids of all."

As Father, I recall to mind,
Those kindergarten days.
I urged the kids through all
   the grades,
With "switches"..."prayers"
   ...and "praise."

My family's grown, I'm
   getting old,
But joys just never stop.
This Father's Day, another first,
This year, I'm old
   "GRANDPOP."

Then there's another joy I have,
On Father's Day each year.
The family God has given me,
HIS CHILDREN, they're so dear.

I feel like Dad to all the church,
Your life we get to share.
We share with you your happy
   days,
Your burdens, want to bear.

continued

HAPPY FATHER'S DAY....FROM DAD'S SIDE!

June 16, 1977

Dedicated to my wife, my boys, and my church.....with Love.

Yes, Father's Day's a two-way street,
Not just for kids to show
Respect for dad...and get him gifts,
As year by year they grow.

I think I speak for other dads,
As with our families live.
We thank you for just being there,
And the comfort that you give.

"His Name"

"For unto us a child is born, unto us a son is given; and the government shall be upon is shoulder; and his name shall be called Wonderful, Counselor, the Mighty God, the Everlasting Father, the Price of Peace." (Isaiah 9:6)

For unto us a child is born,
The prophet did foresee.
And unto us a son is given,
One in the same, would be.

The government he would uphold,
His kingdom ever stand.
His righteousness from shore to shore,
In that eternal land.

His name they said was WONDERFUL,
A proper name indeed.
For in a way most wonderful,
He'd meet man's every need.

The prophet said he's COUNSELOR,
He'd show to us the way.
And help us understand the truth,
And lead us day by day.

The MIGHTY GOD, omnipotent,
With healing in his wings.
Would bring salvation to the world,
Of this the angel sings.

He's EVERLASTING FATHER, too,
The God of ages past.
Would come to earth in form of man,
To bring his love so vast.

A PRINCE OF PEACE they said he'd be,
Amid life's toil and strife.
His peace is free to everyone,
Who yield to him their life.

Who is this one of whom we speak,
The prophet did proclaim?
The one of whom the angels sing,
What really is his name?

The gift of God, sent down to man,
In human flesh he came.
The babe of Bethlehem...King of Kings,
And "JESUS" is his name.

12-14-77

"If Jesus Had Not Come"

Have you given thought
Or wondered what,
If JESUS had not come?
Just what would be
Or would NOT be,
Within the hearts of some?

There'd be no Christmas
Day at all,
No season of the year.
No Yuletide songs
Nor gift exchange,
Our weary hearts to cheer.

No "PEACE ON EARTH,
GOOD WILL TOWARD
   MAN,"
No wise men from afar.
No shepherds who
The story told,
No shining Bethlehem star.

But even more,
There'd be no hope,
No message we could bring.
Of GOD'S great love
And sacrifice,
Of which the Angels sang.

No resurrection
Hope we'd have,
No JESUS' blood to save.
No cross—no crown
No hope beyond,
The regions of the grave.

No hope of heaven
With its joys,
No loved ones could we meet.
No gathering with
That Heavenly host,
To sit at JESUS' feet.

'Tis sad to think
These kind of thoughts,
As carols sweet we hum.
But from HIS words
The question rings,
What "IF I HAD NOT COME?"

But CHRIST DID COME
Down to the earth,
The angels sang for joy.
For in a manger
Meek and low,
Was born a baby boy.

GOD'S gift to man,
The PRINCE OF PEACE,
The KING OF KINGS was HE.
To live and die
For all the world,
And that included me!

So lift your voice
And shout aloud,
Let us HIS praises sing.
For CHRIST is come
The HOPE of all,
To HIS salvation bring.

Pastor Fred O. Rice

*Inspired from JESUS Words in
John 15:22
"If I had not come and spoken
unto them,
they had not had sin; but now
they have no
cloak for their sin.*

ISN'T GOD GOOD

It's Christmas Time Again

'Tis Christmas time, again it has come,
Doth make our hearts rejoice.
As songs of gladness fill the air,
And we lift up our voice.

This speaks to us of many things,
Like Wise Men from afar.
Who found the Christ-Child as foretold,
By following Bethlehem's star.

It speaks of Shepherds from the field,
Who heard the angels sing.
It speaks of love, to all the world
As heavenly anthems ring.

Besides the stories we have heard,
With all their charm and lore.
There's something else that comes to mind,
That we've not said before.

"'Tis Christmas time—AGAIN," we say,
This world again speaks out.
It speaks of God, His faithfulness,
In whom we'll never doubt.

"Again" speaks of a year just past,
The seasons all in place.
The stars, the planets in the sky,
All hanging there in space.

"Again" as in the years gone by,
Two-thousand to be sure.
This day will come "again" next year,
If this old world endure.

"AGAIN," "AGAIN," each year to come,
As in the ages past.
Our loving God will never fail,
As long as time shall last.

'Tis Christmas time, oh blessed day,
The joy it brings mankind.
May we this season of the year,
Help others, joy to find.

(Dec. 9, 1983)
Written while having coffee at McDonalds in Carmel

REFLECTIONS

As I reflect on Christus Gardens,
My heart o'er runs with joy.
For here I see my precious Lord,
Depicted from a boy.

My stroll through Bible's wonderland,
Made new the stories old;
I'd heard in years of long ago,
I thrilled to see them told.

They spoke of love from God above,
Who sent down Heaven's best.
To give His life so all mankind,
Could have eternal rest.

From manger scene—to Calvary's cross,
A Savior's love I see.
That gave Himself a sacrifice,
For sinners just like me.

I see such grace—and mercy too,
Compassion in His face.
As there He taught the multitude,
Of how to run life's race.

I feel with Christ the bitter pang,
While sitting with the twelve.
And knowing well that one of them,
That night His life would sell.

The agony while on the cross,
He suffered there alone.
As all His friends—disciples too,
Thought only of their own.

But oh, the thrill that followed death,
The grave could not contain.
Creator of the universe,
He had to live again!

He's now ascended up on high,
To reign—the scriptures say.
But He will come in clouds again,
Just as He went away.

My reflections here they are,
As all these scenes I view.
At Christus Gardens Galleries,
My faith was stirred anew.

THE NEW YEAR

Another year has passed away,
A new one has begun.
New hopes and opportunities,
Some losses and some fun.

We might look back, the year
   now past,
Might worry fuss and fret.
But what's the use, it's history,
Won't even show regret.

Forget those things which are
   behind,
I hear the writer say.
Reach for the things that lie
   ahead,
and "press" from day to day.

I'll never let last year's mistakes,
Rob me of future days.
I'll just endeavor best I can,
To walk in proper ways.

Obey what God's Word says
   to do,
And work with all my might.
I'll seek to win some souls
   to Him,
And do it with delight.

I'll yearn to reach out to the lost,
To save someone from death.
To bring lost sheep into the fold,
As long as I have breath.

I will enjoy the blessings, too,
That come my way each day.
And ask for guidance from
   above,
When skies seem dark and gray.

I'll run the race and faithful be,
Each day of this new year.
His hand on mine to lead the
   way,
I'll never have to fear.

Perhaps some joys will come my
   way,
Or sorrows hard to bear.
Let come what may, I'll give
   God thanks,
For He is always there.

Yes, 1990 lies ahead,
I know not what shall be.
But I will follow where He
   leads,
We'll walk, my Lord and me.

Jan. 2, 1990

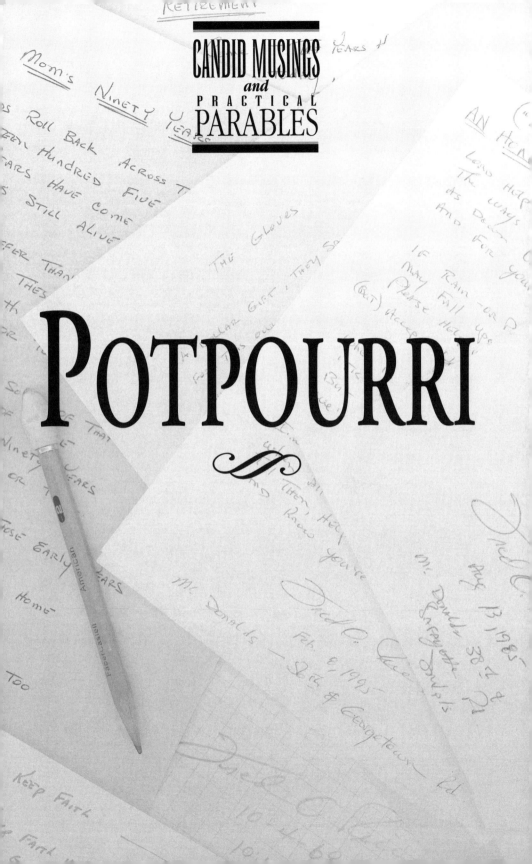

THE TUNER'S LIFE

These lines may not live on
   through years,
As Norman Rockwell's print
But they will be my part tonight,
In this my little stint.

The "TUNER'S LIFE" as I have
   lived,
For almost thirty years.
I offer now as best I can,
To you my cherished peers.

Some years ago I made a choice,
Discussed it with my wife.
I said "one thing I'd like to do,
That's try a TUNER'S LIFE."

I sent for books and hammer
   too,
C-fork and long felt strip.
I've got it all...so here I go,
My life's a brand new trip.

By lesson three I said, "I've
   learned
My fourths and fifths...I think,".
Now looking back, the truth is
   this,
My tuning...it did stink.

A Legion Post in Terre Haute,
The first I tuned for pay.
To think of that poor tuning job,
I shudder yet today.

To justify such shoddy work,
I offer this defense.
My charge was only eight small
   bucks,
And I didn't have much sense.
This life's been fun and now
   I know,
There's more to learn than thirds.
Yet pleasure that's derived from
   it,
Is hard to put in words.

Some things I like, I'll try to
   share,
In these few words of rhyme.
I can't tell all...it's far too much,
Don't really have the time.

I like the FOLKS I get to meet,
A most congenial lot.
They offer cokes and coffee too,
When the weather's cold or hot.

I like my TIME, it's all my own,
My schedule I can make.
Vacation time when e'er I want,
And days off I can take.

Sometimes it's true, the hours
   are long,
But only if I choose.
To make more cash, or
   compensate,
So business I won't lose.

continued

I like the INCOME over all, though
I'll never wealthy be.
For I can't tune enough each week,
To make me rich you see.

I like those FUNNY LITTLE THINGS,
That people always say.
Like "Fifteen years since last 'twas tuned,
Is it very bad today?"

Or, "Does this sweeper bother you,
Don't mind the stereo."
And, "I'll just watch a TV show,
For you won't care I know."

A Steinway or a Melodigrand,
No other job around
Can offer such variety,
Or diversity be found.

Now as the year draws to a close,
I like to reminisce.
Those times of fun and happiness,
Might even call them bliss.

And as we face year '91,
That's quickly drawing near,
I wish you "HAPPY HOLIDAYS"
And a prosperous New Year.

P.S. For those aspiring as I did,
A "TUNER'S LIFE" to live,
A few small words I pass along,
And this advice I give.

Be honest always with yourself,
And honest with all men
Then give your best in all you do;
New clients you will win.

Written 12-5-81
FOR: The Indpls. Chapter
PTG Christmas Party 12-9-81

A Diamond in the Rough

I walked the streets, I viewed the men,
Saw stress upon each face.
I sensed that sin had bound each one,
They'd failed in life's rough race.

As I was want to turn my back,
I felt I'd seen enough.
I saw each man in different light,
A diamond in the rough.

"A Diamond In The Rough," I said,
Great value hid away.
And I would leave such hidden wealth,
To die and just decay?

"What should I do," I asked myself,
"To lift those fallen men?"
For they must know that Jesus' blood,
Can wash away their sin.

This will I do, I'll take time out,
I'll leave the rush behind,
And stretch my hand to needy souls,
So they new hope can find.

I'll tell them of someone who loves,
I'll help them Christ to see.
For lest by grace, from God above,
That fallen man is ME.

Sept. 30, 1977

Growing Old

"Once I was young
Now I am old,"
The Psalmist David said.
And growing old
Through all our life,
Must be our greatest dread.

We pass our teens
Become full grown,
Launch out in life full blast.
Not knowing then
How sweet the years,
Of this brief life are past.

Our twenties come
And soon pass by,
Our thirties come and go.
We hit the forties,
Try to joke,
Those years just won't go slow.

We head for fifty
With some grief,
Each day a brand new page.
Console ourselves
By telling all,
"Now wisdom comes with age."

But all the time
Down deep inside,
We know old age is a fact;
We try to hide
Our feelings true,
By using poise and tact.

As sixty's come
We reminisce,
Those days of youth gone by.
We groan inside
While thinking back,
How swiftly time does fly.

Relive our childhood
Then our teens,
Recall our wedding day.
Our children came
To grace our home,
And now they've gone their way.

Recall our strength,
Vitality;
Our work, we loved it so.
Now we are weak
Can't run the race,
Our muscles from us go.

Ecclesiastes
Chapter 12,
We read what comes with years.
One's vision dimmed
Desire has gone,
And time has plugged his ears.

The keepers of
The house - our hands,
Now tremble and move slow.
The music in
A noisy street,
Now quiet, faint and low.

Three score and ten
Shall man's time be,
No guarantee of more.
For after that
Might someday find,
Death knocking on your door.

September 1, 1985

HUNTING

I'm on my way to shoot a bear,
Or moose or elk or deer.
Some fish—small game—just anything,
That happens to be near.

Now some have said, it's all in vain,
And waste of money too.
But all will see, when we return,
Our game we'll show to you.

Those bear skin rugs and venison,
Will make your eyes pop out.
And when you see that big moose head,
I know you'll have to shout.

And not to speak of all the fish,
The partridge, grouse and quail.
My hopes are high—my faith is strong,
You'll see—we will not fail.

In visions now I see that feast,
A cookout for the host.
A barbecue that just won't quit,
Yes, it will be the most.

Now, just in case, that bear ain't there,
Or the moose sly like a fox.
Or the deer all run and fish don't bite,
Our feast will be—from a box.

10-4-68

MY POTTY-CHAIR

I've tried to learn in every case,
No matter just how grave.
To try and see the brighter side,
Instead of rant and rave.

For case in point, I now refer,
To my past seven days.
In ICU, that dreadful place,
I just don't "dig" their ways.

I stood the needles and the wires,
The pain I seemed to bear.
But one thing most, I hate of all,
Was that blame "Potty-chair."

The food was awful, but I lived,
No washing of my hair.
But even that was not as bad,
As that old "Potty-chair."

No privacy could one enjoy,
The windows were so bare.
As there I sat before the world,
Upon my "Potty-chair."

The nurses said, "it ain't so bad,"
You know that we don't care.
It's part of life you've got to live,
You need that "Potty-chair."

I'd lay as long as nature let,
I'd question, "do I dare?"
And then at last I'd have to call,
For my little "Potty-chair."

Sometimes the pain came oh so strong,
I'd call for that old chair.
And by the time I got all set,
All that would come was air.

I called the nurse 'bout noon one day,
This time the case was rare.
She made my bed, while there I sat,
Upon my "Potty-chair."

From day to day, I'd reason out,
"To me this just ain't fair."
And then the "bed pan" crossed my mind,
I said, "I'll take the chair."

The days soon passed, they moved me from,
The IC Ward back there.
And to my horror came along,
My faithful "Potty-chair."

continued

Just why they sent it, I don't
  know,
"Please, keep it," was my
  prayer.
For in my room I had a bath,
"Don't need that "Potty-chair."

It's all now past, but this I say,
"Just don't you ever dare
To make a Christmas gift to me,
of a "Crazy Potty-Chair!"

Dedicated to the "B-Wing, ICU"
Westview Hospital, Indianapolis
04/11/76

SPRING IN INDIANA

You hear folks sing of spring each year,
Like "Spring Time in the Rockies,"
Or tell of "April in Paris,"
Or the Derby with its jockeys.

But nothing yet can e'er compare,
With spring in Indiana.
Just listen close and you will see,
It's better than Vienna.

Lets start up north, the lake and dunes,
No beauty can compare.
That singing sand along the shore,
It holds a beauty rare.

Then drive on down through farming land,
With corn, soy beans and wheat.
Some corn, some oats, some other crops,
It's surely hard to beat.

The Circle City, what a place,
Variety abounds.
With sports—arts—classics
And famed race track,
In May make mighty sounds.

Let's go on down through winding roads,
Renowned Brown County hills.
The foliage there in colors mixed,
With joy your being fills.

Yet that's not all, there's more to see,
Along the southern part;
Ohio River wide and clear,
All this is just the start.

Yes, Indiana is the place,
Far better than the rest.
It has the mountains and the beach,
Is full from east to west.

I know no state in all the land,
With variety such as this.
For spring like none you've seen before,
Indiana you must not miss.

5-12-88
Hardees - Indianapolis
62nd and Allisonville

THE BEAST

We've heard since 1942,
About a highway rare.
The mighty ALCAN was the name,
For those who travel there.

This road's a challenge, to be sure,
Like none you've ever seen.
Unlike the highways in the States,
That are always paved and clean.

"THE BEAST" I'll call it as I drive,
O'er all its grit and grime.
1,000 miles...and more dirt road,
Are there for you to find.

Just like a BEAST, it has a mind,
To devour all its prey.
You see the signs and evidence,
Strewn all along the way.

There are tires and rims, and bits of scrap,
Wrecked trucks and trailers too.
Stalled campers and some motor homes,
And often with their crew.

The word is trouble if you dare,
To wrestle with the Beast.
Its mountains, rocks and gravel roads,
Are sure to bring its feast.

Though most of this the tourist knows,
The risk he wants to take.
To say, "I drove the Alcan,"
If just for ego sake.

The Beast we tackled, like the rest,
Alaska was in sight.
But lurking down the road not far,
It waited with its might.

It struck at us from time to time,
We fought along the way.
We wrestled it with all our strength,
While traveling day by day.

Our hitch, a tire, some broken glass,
A bumper weld to break.
Those semi trucks and flying rocks,
Are sure their toll to take.

We have some marks and battle
   scars,
To show we had the flight.
We'd ne'er give up or dare turn
   back,
We faced it with our might.

Our flight is over with the Beast,
The battle we have won.
We'll leave behind the Alcan way,
With rising of the sun.

But for the traveler yet to come,
A warning I would give.
"BEWARE THE
   BEAST"....who come this
   way,
If you desire to live.

8-5-77

THE DENTIST

As I recall the days of yore,
One thing rings loud and clear.
My dental visits as a child,
That rolled around each year.

As I would sit down in the chair,
I'd hear the dentist say
"Now this won't hurt, not very
  much,"
And then he'd go his way.

When he returned he had his
  drill,
And big long needle too.
My heart beat fast, my stomach
  churned,
I knew what he would do.

The drill seemed louder in those
  days,
The novocaine didn't work.
The drill would slip and hit the
  nerve,
And I would twitch and jerk.

This is a fact, I kid you not,
I still can feel the pain.
I vowed if I should ere grow up,
I'd never go again.

I tried to keep that promise made,
And almost made it too.
For dental visits as a man,
Have been quite short and few.

As I grew older through the years,
I'd hear some people say.
It's all been changed since
  yesteryear,
It's not so bad today.

Past forty years since vow was
  made,
My heart it softened some.
And since my teeth were
  needing work,
I felt the time had come.

With apprehension to be sure,
I went down to the school
Where dental work is done for
  less,
I must have been a fool.
We talked it over, made a list,
Of all that needed done.
'Twould take some time to do it all,
I questioned, should I run?

I was assigned to student doc,
Now Jamie was her name.
I knew not then, by time she's
  done,
I'd never be the same.

She took full x-rays of my mouth,
I coughed and gagged a bit.
But did my best to be a man,
As in the chair I sit.

A time was set to start my work,
Knew not what was in store.
From drilling...filling...root canal,
All this and plenty more.

She checked my teeth, yes every one,
I think she liked to drill.
As one by one from front to back,
Each tooth she had to fill.

That rubber dam, I thought I'd die,
I'd smother...gasp for air.
I'd try my best to act grown-up,
And at the ceiling stare.

Then came the time to do my gums,
She'd scrape down to the bone.
I'd fight the tears and act real brave,
While deep inside I'd groan.

A minor surgery on my gums,
"Now this won't hurt too bad."
I heard those words long years ago,
When I was just lad.

A "drill" instructor did the work,
He really looked the part.
We called him "Sarge,"
(not to his face)
He seemed to have no heart.

We then moved on, the work progressed,
New bridges were in sight.
I knew I'd live now after all,
The days were looking bright.

But Wait! A problem then arose,
Here's what the teacher said.
"I see a blushing on that tooth,
A Root Canal ahead."

That made my day, and Jamie's too,
We both were feeling low.
But what's to do, we've come this far,
So forward we must go.

I'll not enlarge on this event,
'twas not of great delight.
But in a project such as this,
Things really must be right.

We now proceed, impressions made,
Then made...and made again.
Was tempted to say words not nice,
But knew that would be sin.

Instructors differed time to time,
The work was moving slow.
I got upset, 'bout blew my cool,
I let the teacher know.

As last, we got a bridge put in,
For Christmas '85.
Two years had passed up to this point,
And I was still alive.

One bridge now in, just four to go,
There's progress to be sure.
I'd stick it out however long,
The rest I could endure.

continued

The months passed by the work was done,
Gold bridges one by one.
Till five in all were in my mouth,
At last it all was done!

A word 'bout JAMIE I would make,
A freshman when we met.
Her Senior year is now complete,
Her graduation set.

A Tribute here I wish to give,
To Jamie, She's the most!
And for my work she's done so well,
I drink to her a toast.

I wish for her, along with Mark,
And little Ryan too.
God's best in all their days ahead,
And everything they do!

There's just one thing I'd like to add,
PLEASE LET THE RECORD SHOW.
A DENTIST HURTS AS MUCH TODAY,
AS FORTY YEARS AGO!

May 5, 1987
Dedicated with great appreciation to Jamie who worked patiently with me through all four years of her dental college.
May '84 through May '87

THE GLOVES

A dollar gift, they said to buy,
For this our gift exchange.
But what's to get—such small
    amount,
Not much in that price range.

But then I found these little
    gloves,
Your pinkies they should fit.
One size fits all, they seem to be,
They're sure to make a hit.

They're quite petite and pretty
    too,
Are nice and warm I'd think.
Bright red will also catch your
    eye,
Might almost make you blink.

BUT —

If you don't like them, don't
    feel bad,
To pass them on is okay.
Or tuck them in a drawer
    somewhere,
In memory of this day.

12-10-95

THE SAGA OF A CADILLAC

While driving west out Plainfield way
One bright and cheery autumn day,
I saw a car that caught my eye,
To own one like it was my cry.

A Cadillac, though not brand new,
A Fleetwood Brougham, year '82.
A cream-puff car in every way,
I vowed to own one, come...some day.

Computer readout on the dash,
Change seat positions in a flash.
It had the extras...every one,
If I could own one, oh what fun.

I took my wife to see this car,
It had not dent, nor scratch, nor mar.
We asked the price, near 11 Thou,
But they'd come down; 10,500, right now.

We said we'd wait and think a bit,
While everything inside me lit.
A week passed by, my wife away,
Up on the farm with Mom to stay.
When she got back we went to see,
Would it be sold or there for me?
To my delight, had not been sold,
By now my hopes were waxing bold.

We dickered more about the cost,
Could deal be made or deal be lost?
We came to terms, 10,300 was it,
We drove the car and in it sit.

We made the deal, did papers sign,
I knew right then, it'd soon be mine.
We took the manual, went our way,
We'd pick it up on 'morrow day.

I cleaned the garage and cleared
   a place,
So there would be an ample
   space.
To keep it sheltered from the
   snow,
That's sure to come with
   winter's blow.
But all that night my wife didn't
   sleep,
Awake 'ere dawn in sorrows
   deep.
She'd changed her mind, no joy
   was there,
Didn't want that car, didn't even
   care.

I knew those feelings couldn't
   last,
An hour or two, they'd soon be
   past.
I went to work all up to par,
'Ere day was done, I'd have
   my car.

When I came home near even
   tide,
To get the car and in it ride.
She said "OH NO! No deal
   for me,
Go break the contract, call
   and see."

We argued some, both feeling
   bad,
Her for the debt, and I was sad.
When reason seemed of no
   avail,
That car with joy, could not
   prevail.

I made the call against my will,
The evening sad and very still.
The salesman yet has not given
   in,
The deal still hangs...things in
   a din.

We'll know today just what
   shall be,
So I will guess and wait and see.
The saga's end will come
   tonight,
When I shall see what is my
   plight.

The above verses were written Friday Nov. 8, 1985 (8:30 a.m.) at a McDonald's restaurant in Kokomo, Indiana before my first appointment that day.

The day is past, soon I shall
   hear,
What verdict falls upon my ear.
A call to make, my insides turn,
As I will soon the answer learn.

We got the word, we've been
   released,
Now Evelyn's stress and sorrow
   ceased.
But I am sad, my hopes have
   fled,
No Cadillac before I'm dead.

It cost some bucks to get us free,
200 plus...that comes from me.
But I'm henpecked, I don't
   deny,
Right now I'd like to sit and cry.

continued

I feel a little bitter, too,
But disappointment isn't new.
To give and take is part of life,
Seems I give more than does my wife.

Now when a Caddy passes my way,
Just listen close, might hear me say,
"To want the best is not a sin."
I'll always think what might have been.

*Poem finished 11-8-85 (4:00 p.m.)
at McDonald's, Northwestern & 56th
Streets.......Indianapolis*

To Lose or Not to Lose

A question I have asked oft times,
"To lose or not to lose?"
Should I be fat? Should I be thin?
Which answer should I choose?

Some facts to face in either case,
Consider both I should.
To make a choice intelligent,
The wisest choice I could.

To shed some lard could help my looks,
Would make my waistline thin.
But in the mirror on the wall,
There's a "gobbler" 'neath my chin.

The doc says it would help my health,
To shed some of my flab.
But when I'm always hungry,
I'm just a mean old crab.

Now if I keep my rolls of fat,
I'm a jolly sort of guy.
Just like a big old teddy bear,
With all my cake and pie.

If I should live to ripe old age,
Ought lose a few more pounds.
But if I'd die before my time,
As well might make my rounds.

I've not decided which I'll choose,
Decision's not in sight.
I'm still a thinkin' 'bout it all,
As these few lines I write.

I've lost some pounds in past few weeks,
Two-twenty use to be.
I've lost the twenty—down to two,
Most anyone can see.

Just how much further I should go,
I've not decided yet.
If I'm "to lose or not to lose,"
You'd best not make a bet.

9-20-83
McDonald's - Carmel
(Between appointments)
(P.S. I only drank coffee!
Refrained from eating)

CANDID MUSINGS *and* PRACTICAL PARABLES

FAMILY

A SMALL SURPRISE

I thought today I'd give to you,
A little small surprise.
By way of line and verse and rhyme,
Before I must arise.

Return to work in moments few,
But 'ere I go my way.
I want to say "I love you, dear,"
This lovely sunny day.

It's been some time since last I wrote,
A poem for my love.
But I still love you just as much,
As sure as heaven's above.

Now I must go on back to work,
It's now nigh unto four.
So bye for now my sweetheart true,
Tonight I'll tell you more.

Love,
Freddie

11/16/65

AMBER

Her hair is blonde,
Her lips are red,
Her cheeks a rosy hue.
A little twinkle
In her eyes,
Like her there's very few.

Her smile is sweet
'Twould melt your heart,
And she's not really mean.
Yet midst the twinkle
And the smile,
Some mischief can be seen.

She likes to play
With Barbie dolls,
She likes to ride her bike.
She likes to join with
Mom and dad,
While going for a hike.

Her grandma helped
Look after her,
She was just a tot.
While mama worked
And went to school,
More education got.

Lakeview Daycare
Held happy days,
With all her friends around.
While playing there
With other kids,
Christ Jesus could be found.

She went to school
Every day,
The smartest in her class.
Next spring when
School term is up,
For sure she's gonna pass.

We've watched her grow
Past seven years,
She's wrapped around our heart.
It brought some tears
We tried to hide,
When from us she must part.

Her room's the same
With little change,
Stuffed toys upon her bed.
"She will return
To visit us,
I know," her grandma said.

Her picture hangs
Upon the wall,
We look at every day.
We miss her so
It breaks our heart,
One hears the grandpa say.

What is the name
Of whom I speak,
I'm sure you ready know.
It's AMBER DAWN
Our first grandchild,
Oh, how we love her so!!!

– Grandpa –

05/31/84 - 11:00 a.m. • McDonald's - Beech Grove

AMBER'S BREAKFAST

Amber likes her "Special K,"
Her favorite breakfast food.
She puts on sugar, milk and cream
And says its very good.

Then next she butters up her toast,
And spreads on jelly thick.
And by the time she gets it down,
It almost makes her sick.

She drinks her milk and water, too
She guzzles it right down.
Then grandpa gives a dirty look,
And grandma makes a frown.

And by this time her belly hurts,
To restroom she must run.
It really isn't quite that bad,
She does it just for fun.

And next it's down into the floor,
The table overhead.
And grandpa gripes about such things,
It makes his face quite red.

It's time to go the food is gone,
And grandpa is quite glad.
But he loves Amber just the same,
If she's good or if she's bad.

Grandpa at Charlie Brown's
1-22-83

AMBER'S TOYS

I know a little Miss,
And Amber is her name.
She's playing all the time,
For life is just a game.

Her "Barbies" are a part,
Of her daily fun and games.
She knows them every one,
And even calls their names.

She has a new-found friend,
That lately to her came.
A turtle nice and green,
But haven't found a name.

She never has enough;
She wants more of the same.
To get another toy,
Now daily is her aim.

But grandma is the one,
Who always gets the blame,
For buying all these toys,
That to her playroom came.

A Boy's Tribute to Mother

I'm just a boy, as tough as some,
But some things I do know.
And one of them, is 'bout my mom,
A lady you should know.

I'd like to pay to her today,
A tribute very true.
For I realize, were it not for her,
My joys would be very few.

No money for expensive gifts,
Have I within my coffer.
But words of tribute from my heart,
With love to her I offer.

She does those things, those little things,
To bring me happiness.
And looks to see if my ears are clean,
And that I properly dress.

Sometimes she yells, but I don't mind,
'Cause it's usually for my good.
I know she wants her boys to be,
As good as good boys should.

So "MOTHER DEAR" to you I say,
With all my heart and soul.
I love you now; I'll love you more,
As years along do roll.

Now please receive with open heart,
This tribute that I give.
And may each day bring happiness,
As long as you shall live.

P.S. "I LOVE YOU"

1962

Christmas Coming Late

Your Christmas gift is yet to come,
We're sorry it is late.
But though we tried to get it here,
They couldn't make the date.

We'll let you guess just what it is,
That you might want yet more,
Now start your brain and think real hard,
What you are waiting for.

A hint or two we'll pass your way,
To help you try and know,
Without some help you'd never guess,
Your spirits would be low.

It's not too large, but big enough
To meet a certain need,
Been quite a problem to secure,
Expensive...yes indeed!

Now you can use it in your work,
Though not used every day.
You'll need to learn just how it works,
You might not know the way.

Composed of several different parts,
Yet all fit into one.
To do the job, professionally,
The best you've ever done.

Must we proceed...or have you guessed,
What this small gift might be?
A little jewel, to be sure,
Now just you wait and see.

Now here's a clue, and you can't miss,
To guess this handy tool.
Your friends will see it in your hand,
They'll all just stand and drool.

You use it on the sounding
   board,
To open up the crack.
It makes your cut, precision
   clean,
You can't get off the track.

Yes, its the ROUTER that
   you want,
We know it's on the way.
We hope that it's worth
   waiting for,
With that, now let us say........

MERRY CHRISTMAS! ! !
Po and Mo

CHRISTMAS EVE

It's Christmas Eve of '92,
Things not the same it seems.
No hustle-bustle as years
 now past,
Can only recall dreams.

Remember now the days
 gone by,
When I was just a boy.
We'd open gifts on
 Christmas Eve,
If it was just a toy.

In later years as I grew up,
And took to me a wife.
We'd always wait for
 Christmas Eve,
'Twas just a part of life.

Remember well in '48,
My folks lived in Brazil.
We waited up for June and
 Marsh,
Our Christmas Eve to fill.

Then later years our sons were
 born,
They brought such joy and bliss.
On Christmas Eve we opened
 gifts,
With so much happiness.

I well recall in Terre Haute,
The boys not yet sixteen.
They got a cycle on that year,
More joy I've never seen.

Some years we went up on the
 farm,
Had Christmas Eve that way.
Sometimes stayed home to open
 gifts,
'Fore going Christmas Day.

Sometimes 'twas church on
 Christmas Eve,
Cantata or a Play.
Sometimes taking gifts to needy
 folks,
And "Merry Christmas" say.

Tonight it's different from the
 past,
This evening isn't fun.
The family all have gone their
 way,
Excitement—there is none.

We tried to watch some TV
 shows,
There really wasn't much.
Some old reruns we'd seen before,
Of Scrooge and likes of such.

By nine o'clock our night was
   o'er,
Our Christmas Eve was past.
'Twas time for bed, least seemed
   that way,
This night just like the last.

I'm not complaining 'bout it all,
Just musing—days of yore.
I know things change as time
   goes by,
Can't stay as years before.

We know when 'morrow
   sunlight breaks,
'Twill bring a Christmas Day.
We'll see our family—least part
   of them,
And "Merry Christmas" say.

Then all the gloom this
   Christmas Eve,
Will vanish with the night.
And Christmas Day of '92,
Will cheery be and bright!

I'll now retire and get some rest,
With this, shut out my light.
I'm feeling better—even now,
I'll say to all—"Good Night".

12/24/92
(around 9:30 p.m., finished around 11:00)

DEAR MO

You like a note,
So here you are
To tell you of my day.
I tuned the church,
And came back home,
My future plans to lay.

I'm on my way,
To tune two more,
Near 12th and Alabam'.
The new "Young Chang,"
Is what they are,
I'll do them like whiz-bam.

Then on to school,
Harcourt I guess,
There should be five or six.
But if I'm tired,
And all pooped out,
I'll quit and tell them "Nix".

The clock is now
Just striking 10,
I must be on my way.
I'll see you then
When 'ere I'm done,
At closing of the day.

I love you much,
With all my heart,
Love more than I can say.
I'll be with you,
Through thick and thin,
So smile, have a good day.

Po
12/04/80

Forty Years of Happiness

We've flown away
To celebrate,
Our Anniversary Day.
'Tis forty years
The twenty-fifth,
They've swiftly passed away.

I well recall
That day in June,
Of nineteen-forty-eight.
I met you dear
My heart did leap,
Must've been the hand of fate.

Our eyes would meet
From time to time,
Toward you my feelings went.
In just one week
I knew that for
Each other we were meant.

Remember well
That girl in white,
One Sunday afternoon.
Express my feelings,
Should I dare?
This seemed a bit too soon.

The week that followed
We did talk,
Expressed our love to each.
'Twas automatic
As we talked,
For you my arms did reach.

That summer seemed
To go so fast,
In other ways quite slow.
I counted
Every single day,
When to my love I'd go.

September came
The day arrived,
And I was on my way.
To take my love
Awaiting me,
This was our wedding day.

The family gathered
In your home,
Just as we planned ahead.
The wedding small
As we had wished,
The ceremony read.

So much has happened
'Cross the years,
With joys, yes, sorrows, too.
But when compared,
The joys outweighed,
The sorrows have been few.

You gave me sons
Each father's dream,
His to carry on.
A mother true
You proved to be,
Was up oft long 'fore dawn.

As pastor's wife
You stood by me,
When sometimes deep inside,
You'd rather run
The other way,
Or go some place and hide.

Besides our home
You kept intact,
You worked a job as well.
On top of that
Your church work came,
Oft times too much to tell.

There's so much more
That comes to mind,
While looking back through
    years.
Some things, they bring me
Laughter—and
Some things, they bring me tears.

But whether joy or tears
With thanks my heart overflows.
You're still with me,
And in good health,
Our love today still glows.

How many years
Still be ahead,
Is surely in God's hands.
But just as long
As we both live,
My love for you will stand.

So come on now
Let's celebrate,
This Anniversary trip.
And as a toast
To forty years,
A little champagne sip.

FRIDAY WORK

Dear Mo, (6:30 a.m.)

I got me up
Some time past six,
And thought I'd first
My breakfast fix.

Then said "Oh no"
I'll not do that,
For I'm already
Much too fat.

I took the sheets
Off of the bed,
To make it clean
As you had said.

I put them in
The washing tub,
While I did in
The shower scrub.

While sheets were getting
Dry and soft,
I swept the floor
Of all its dross.

The dust rag, too
I used it some,
So things were clean
When home you'd come.

The kitchen I
Did not get done,
And family room
It still needs some.

But what I've done
I trust will be,
A help to you
From little "me."

Po

P.S. (8:00 a.m.)
The kids room
And my office, too,
I closed the door
And did not do.

It's really not much
I have done,
But trust approval
I have won.

I'm drinking now
A cup of brew,
While orders fix
And think of you!!

In all seriousness,
I do love you with
All my heart.

I hope the little
I did this a.m.,
Will be of some
Help to you.

Love,
Po

HAPPY ANNIVERSARY DEAR

I'll keep my word
Not get a card,
As we agreed to do.
But I must say
In some small way,
I'm still in love with you.

So here's some word
Set down in rhyme,
To say "I love you, Dear,"
And pray as years
May come and go,
I'll have you always near.

Since "forty-eight"
There's been so much,
That's come and gone with years.
There's been a lot
That's brought us joy,
And some has brought us tears.

If I should try
To write in part,
Of all that's passed our way.
"Twould fill a book
Yes, maybe two,
And I'd be here all day.

But most of all
This special date,
I simply wish to say.
Above our love
Of yesteryear,
I Love You More Today!

Now I could add
More lines of rhyme,
To these that I have done.
But I could never
Add more love,
To You, my only one.

So on our
Anniversary Day,
Here's love with all my heart.
And trust till Jesus
Takes us both,
We'll never have to part.

With all my love,
Freddie
September 25, 1948
September 25, 1984

KEEP FAITH

Keep faith, my love, and don't despair,
Our God is on your side.
Though clouds be dark and it may seem,
His loving face they hide.

For just beyond those rolling clouds,
That bring to us the storm.
His smiling face is still up there,
Your broken heart to warm.

The darkest hour is just before,
The sun comes breaking through.
So don't give up—keep holding on,
To God—HE STILL LOVES YOU!

Yes, at this special time of year,
When hearts should sing with joy.
I know your heart is weighted down,
For one—your baby boy.

But in God's Word, I read of one,
Who likewise erred away
(Luke 15);
But he came home a different boy,
And never more did stray.

Now lift your head, and weary heart,
Let God your helper be.
He'll give you strength, this Christmas time, and
Remember—you still have me.

There're others near who need your help,
Levi and Cheryl too—
There're Courtney, Amber and your folks
For them some things must do.

So let's agree, as in God's Word,
His strength is guaranteed
(Psalm 46)
To lift you up and see you through,
And meet your every need.

With Love,
Po

12/16/80

LIFE AIN'T FAIR

Sometimes it seems
That life ain't fair,
When looking o'er one's lot.
Things not wanted
Come to pass,
Things longed for just are not.

One looks for health
And wealth and things,
To comfort 'long life's way.
But health, it breaks
And wealth don't come,
We struggle day to day.

A case in point,
I just went through,
Trip of a lifetime won.
Expenses paid, no cost to me,
Oh Boy!—it sounded fun.

My plans were made
My bags were packed,
I even bought some Yen.
To make a trip
So big as this,
Japan, I'd never been.

The night before
I was to leave,
My plans came crashing down.
I found myself
In ambulance,
And speeding 'cross the town.

How can this happen
Was my cry,
It seems that life ain't fair.
The plane took off
I'm not on board,
At hospital walls I stare.

But as a Christian
I must say,
My life is in God's hand.
Our steps are ordered
By the Lord,
Though we don't understand.

I'll not be bitter
'bout it all,
Must see the brighter side.
Though all the answers
Are not clear,
Some things He'll from us hide.

True—Life ain't fair
But well—So what,
There's little can be changed.
So I'll go on
Keep looking up,
Though plans get rearranged.

A trip I'll take
One day I'm sure,
Much better, one must say.
Not just the Land
of Rising Sun,
But of Eternal Day !

5-23-89 Wrote at MCL - Lawrence, Ind.
Hardees - Lawrence (re-wrote)

MEMORIES OF DAD

The question often rises,
About this time of year,
"What makes a DAD so special,
What makes us hold him dear?"

The reasons may be many,
The thoughts be varied too.
So the memories of my dad today,
I'd like to share with you.

I see my dad...his stature short,
Stand well above the rest,
It was his life that made it so.
I felt he was the best.

He worked as hard as any man,
With callous on his hand.
Yet tenderly, he'd touch my head,
As by my side he'd stand.

He managed well on little,
When times were hard and rough.
He never did disparage,
But said, "there'll be enough."

He knew the days of sunshine,
When better times came 'round.
And thanked the Lord for blessing,
When plenty did abound.

He knew the power of praying,
And trusting God to lead.
Of looking to the Bible,
In every time of need.

This little man could preach, too,
With vigor and with zeal;
The saving power of Jesus,
Conviction you would feel.

Both time and space would fail me,
To tell of all the rest.
Suffice it all to say though,
For such a dad... I'm blest.

The years have come and gone now,
But memories linger still.
Of that great man who taught me,
To love, and know God's will.

Today I think of Dad again,
With hallowed thoughts and sweet.
And purpose there in heaven,
One day with Christ, we'll meet.

By Rev. Fred O. Rice in living memory and dedicated to all who share the memory of their fathers who have gone on before.

June 16, 1974

Mom's Ninety Years

Our minds roll back across the years,
To nineteen hundred five.
Yes ninety years have come and gone,
And Mom is still alive.

For this we offer thanks to God,
Whose given her these years.
And given strength for every day,
Come happiness or tears.

We'd like to share some of that life,
In these few words of rhyme.
Can't cover much of ninety years,
Don't have the space or time.

But let's start back, those early years,
When she was just a babe.
Who brightened up the Randles' home,
She joy and sparkle gave.

She had some sisters, brothers too,
Frank—Melvin—Alice—Grace.
They all made up this happy home,
But none took "Stella's" place.

Of school days—we're not too sure,
But this much we do know.
She never failed or missed a grade,
As through those years did go.

She'd graduate in '24,
West Lebanon the town.
Back then girls made their special dress,
They had no cap and gown.

With school days past, and life ahead,
A young adult was she.
A job was needed—to be sure,
So self-reliant she could be.

Mom might have been an
  early start,
Of what we know today
As "Women's-Lib"—or
  something near,
When she went to work for pay.

At Farmers Bank, the teller
  there,
Had always been a man.
But Mom broke the ice and
  took the job,
She showed a woman can!!

As time passed by, like any lass,
A family crossed her mind.
A man and children she could
  love,
And in due time would find.

Among the many boys
  mom met,
She may have choosy been.
Not in a hurry—she would wait,
Her heart would tell her when.

And then one day "HE"
  came along,
Now Levi was his name.
It wasn't long until she knew,
Their hearts were much the
  same.

In course of time proposal made,
To which Mom did agree.
The wedding bells were soon to
  ring,
A "June bride" she would be.

Now June the ninth, that was the
  day,
In nineteen twenty-eight.
They took their vows and
  pledged their love,
They each had found their mate.
God blessed this union and their
  home,
With children through the years.
Saw four grow up to be adults,
Lost four—thus bringing tears.

Now Mom worked hard through
  all those years,
The house—the kids—the farm.
Helped Dad with chores and
  milking cows,
But never lost her charm.

We spoke of loss that brought
  her grief,
Four babies did not live.
Then Alice died in later years,
Mom found peace God can give.

She learned ones help comes
  from above,
That God is always there.
She taught these truths in
  Sunday School,
God's Word she loved to share.

Might mention here the Hedrick
  Church
Adult class that she taught.
Some 40 years—or there about,
Brought joy that can't be
  bought.

continued

The joy she felt was not just
   hers,
But others through the years.
Found from her teaching,
   happiness
And freedom from their cares.

And yet today, within her heart,
That church has special place.
For there she found her Lord
   so dear,
And His redeeming grace.

Mom can't attend as days of
   yore,
Her body's frail and weak.
But Sunday morn she asks for
   strength,
To go—and blessing seek.

The years have passed, some
   things have changed,
And Dad has been called home.
It's now ten years since he has
   gone,
And Mom was left alone.

"Alone"—that's not the best of
   words,
For Jesus is her friend.
He's always there in time of need,
To strength and comfort lead.

And then she has her family too,
Three daughters here abide.
Evelyn—Naomi—Lenora Mae,
They're always by her side.

Just what the Lord still has in
   store,
For Mom, these next few years.
It's in His hands and providence,
She'll face it without fears.

God's Word has said He'll not
   forsake,
Nor leave her stand alone.
From day to day He'll be her
   strength,
Until He calls her home!!

*(Matthew 28:20 says "And lo I am
with you always, even unto the end
of the world")*

*Written for Evelyn's mother (Estella
Cronkhite) for her 90th Birthday
September 30, 1995*

A Mother's Day Tribute

Another Mother's Day has come,
Just like in days gone by.
As I reflect on those now past,
I marvel—time does fly.

Remember I was just a kid,
I'd come to Mother dear,
To wish her well on Mother's Day;
We'd hold each other near.

As years moved by on Mother's Day,
That day had meaning more.
For when I wed the girl I loved,
Another I'd adore.

Not just my wife, but her mom too,
Were now a part of me.
From then each year on Mother's Day,
Not one to love, but three.

Then in a year or two at most,
This day took on new life.
For now the mother of my child,
Was more than just my wife.
The years have passed—now thirty five,
My life grows more each day.
And every year I've tried to show,
The truth in what I say.

Oft times 'twas small, the gift I gave,
But it came from my heart.
I trust she knew on Mother's Day,
My love would never part.

I'm growing old—that's what they say,
When one does reminisce.
But looking back on Mother's Days,
Brings happiness and bliss.

continued

I honor Mom whose gone before,
I'll cherish memories dear.
My mom-in-law I'll honor too,
While God does keep her here.

But most of all this Mother's Day,
A tribute I would make.
To one whose been a mother true,
She lived for "others" sake.

She took the role of "Mother Dear,"
While yet in tender years.
Nineteen was young for such a task,
But faced it without fears.

By twenty-one she's mother twice,
Was mother of the year.
The youngest mother in the church,
Thoughts almost bring a tear.

She had another role to fill,
For thirty years or so.
As mother of the church, you know,
Wherever we would go.

The years have passed, our boys are grown,
And each one gone his way.
Her Mom's grown old through passing time,
My Mom's in heaven today.

Now on this day, it's only us,
To look back 'cross the years.
And think of Mother's Days gone by,
While holding back our tears.

To her, my love—this Mother's Day,
A tribute may I give.
The greatest mother of all time,
As long as she shall live.

Her name is "Frances Evelyn Rice,"
Her boys there call her "Mo;"
With tender love—affection too,
This day we love her so!

With All My Love

Mother's Day
1984
Freddie

MOTHER

My mind goes back
Across the years,
To times that were so sweet.
When MOTHER DEAR
Would call us kids,
To sit around her feet.

She told us all
Those Bible tales,
Of giants and of bears.
She told us too
Of Jesus sweet,
Who would drive away
   the cares.

Such sacred thoughts,
Those blessed days,
I love to reminisce.
Just stop and think
Of all those joys,
Such happiness and bliss.

The years flew by,
We found ourselves
With families of our own.
And prayed the seed
Of MOTHER'S faith,
In our children's heart be sown.

The faith that MOTHER
Lived and taught,
It kept her through the years.
It eased the heartache,
Pain and loss,
It drove away the fears.

That faith undimmed
Through darkened nights,
Will have reward I'm sure.
For Jesus promised
Heaven's joys,
To MOTHERS just like her.

Mom's house on earth,
It's now dissolved,
Her trials are all o'er.
The sorrows, tears
And pains of life
Will burden her no more.

"For we know,"
The writer said,
"This earthly house shall fade.
But one that can't
Be built with hands,
For eternity is made."

continued

In that new home,
Where Mom now lives,
All tears are wiped away.
With only joy
And happiness,
In that eternal day.

With vision bright
She looks upon,
The face of Jesus sweet.
And strength of youth
She now enjoys,
While sitting at His feet.

But best of all,
With hearing keen,
Her ears unstopped and clear.
She's heard "WELL DONE,
You've run the race,
At last my child you're here."

And now with Dad
And those gone on,
She's joined that happy band.
To live forever
Over there,
In that celestial land.

We would not want
To call her back,
From heaven's golden shore.
For a crown of Life
And that white stone,
Are hers forevermore.

Just one desire
I now possess,
As David said before.
"She'll not return
To us on earth,
But we shall go to her."

In loving memory of my mother who passed from this life on May 8, 1972 in my home. The fore part of this poem, I wrote to her for Mother's Day 1960. I revised it to fit into the words which came to me while in the hotel the day of her funeral. The poem was completed on Mother's Day, May 14, 1972.

MY DEARLY BELOVED

My dearly beloved,
The charm of my life.
My only true love,
My dear precious wife.

I've tried through the years,
My love to display.
Though oft' it has been,
In a poor and weak way.

This year I desire,
Something special to do.
A gift far excelling,
My others to you.

I trust you'll accept it,
With all of my heart.
And keep it forever,
From it never part.

To find this gift special,
To the clock you must go.
Then open the door,
And feel down below.

Then bring what you find,
Down under the tree.
And open your gift,
Especially from me.

With all my love,
Freddie

Christmas 1977

MY SIS

The day, October twenty-five,
The year was nineteen-twelve.
A baby girl brought happiness,
To a home where she would dwell.

"ODESSA MAE" would be her name,
Like music it did ring.
The parents young, were filled with joy,
Such pleasure she did bring.

Her days of childhood quickly passed,
The years they came and went.
And all the time, these parents knew,
From heaven she was sent.

A normal girl in every way,
She played with dolls and toys.
And as she grew, her interests change,
Attention went to boys.

She met a guy named "LOWELL GRAVES,"
In proper course of time.
She set her cap, and said "for sure,
Now this young man is mine."

God blessed this union, to be sure,
Their children numbered five.
A happy home with joy and love,
That truly would survive.

It's sad to say, dark days oft' come,
With clouds...and some with rain.
The songs and laughter, joy and bliss,
Sometimes give way to pain.

Life's sorrows come, in difference ways,
In sickness, stress and woe.
Sometimes its death that bring us tears,
As loved ones from us go.

My Sis Odessa's seen it all,
As God called Lowell home.
There with five children left to raise,
She faced the world alone.

But with a faith that would not quit,
She said, "I must press on."
For God has promised in his Word,
"After darkness comes the dawn" (Psalm 30:5).

Her faith was honored by the Lord,
God knew her every need.
He sent support to bear the load,
And help her family feed.

Yes, you might know of whom I speak,
"GUS CONTAT" was the man.
Who came her way, and fit right in,
To God's appointed plan.

He took Odessa to himself,
The kids, just as his own.
His love, support and strength he gave,
Until he saw them grown.

Odessa's faith has long remained,
Unto this very day.
God's ways are best, in joy or pain,
We often hear her say.

A favorite motto by her chair,
She reads from time to time.
"Nevertheless Thy Will be done,
My will be lost in Thine."

The years have passed, she's not as spry,
Her hearing not as keen.
As in some years that now are gone,
Or days that she has seen.

But in her heart, she's youthful still,
She shows to all a love.
That won't grow old, for it was sent,
From God in heaven above.

Yes, that's MY SIS, one of a kind,
We really love her so.
And pray for MANY BIRTHDAYS MORE,
Before God says "Let's go."

With all my love!
Freddie

8-8-92

My New Year's Resolution 1974

There are resolutions, I have made,
For New Year's of the past.
Then none were made for other years,
'Cause I knew they'd not last.

But for the year that lies ahead,
Being nineteen seventy-four.
I'll try again to make a pledge,
Just one...then nothing more.

It's to my wife I give my word,
To her I make my vow.
I'll keep my promise just you see,
Though confess I don't know how.

Now hold your hat and keep your seat,
While I tell you this strange tale.
What to expect this coming year,
And hope I will not fail.

I PROMISE YOU I'LL NOT SPEAK BAD,
About or to you dear.
No unkind word with you inferred,
Will you or others hear.

If with your thoughts I don't concur,
Your words I disagree.
I'll hold my tongue and let you go,
To speak your feelings free.

Discriminating words my dear,
Of you I will not seek.
My words will be of high esteem,
Those only will I speak.

This resolution I have made,
Of things I will not say.
I promise you with seal below,
Will start on New Year's Day.

12-30-73

ONE SIZE FITS ALL

As Christmastime drew near this year,
Gift giving came to mind.
We'd purchase gifts for those we love,
But questioned . . . ."What's to find?"

There's Levi...Cheryl...Rita...Fred,
Ann...Eric...Courtney Jo,
And Amber Dawn; What would they like,
Where might we shop or go?

A sweater, shoes, dress, or blue jeans,
We might not find the brand,
(Designer, that is).
A tool for guys, cologne for gals,
That didn't sound too grand.

And then a thought came cross our mind,
One gift that all could use.
The answer clear, "One size fits all,"
Our problem thus defuse.

A gift with color all would like,
Green matching every thing.
Ben Franklin's picture on this gift,
It surely joy would bring.

No matter if you're large or small,
"One size fits all," we said.
Could be in teens...or twilight years,
This works until you're dead.

The riddle you by now have solved,
You've guessed what's in your gift.
We trust it adds more
   CHRISTMAS JOY,
And gives to you a lift!

With love,
Mom & Dad

Christmas 1995

Retirement

The years have come—the years have gone,
And here we are today.
Retirement years have slowly crept,
And stretched their arms your way.

It seems like only yesterday,
As 'cross the years we look.
That at the age of "twenty-one,"
Your first position took.

Two babes—a home—a man and church,
Those duties—yes, and more.
You took that job, an evening shift,
Finances to secure.

Near forty years you held a job,
Some not the best, I'd say.
The "Oil Room" on Bloomington,
That "Green House"—not much pay.

A midnight shift in Terre Haute,
For you was not much fun.
Those nights were long—some dreary too,
'Ere rising of the sun.

Some jobs, you rose up early morn,
'Fore breaking of the day.
And headed out to face your task,
'Twas not a pleasant way.

Recall those miles that you drove,
Each day in cold or heat.
From Bedford up to Bloomington,
In rain or snow or sleet.

Then, here in Indy 'cross the town,
Or round the interstate,
'Bout thirty miles either way,
And you were never late.

Some jobs were better, to be sure,
Some had a touch of class.
But through the years, the hope remained,
"These Years of Work Will Pass."

Those years did pass, now here we are,
Mixed feelings I would guess.
A joy to reach "The Golden Years,"
Some sadness nonetheless.

A touch of melancholy—yes,
With memories of the past.
But happiness for years ahead,
And joy that 'ere shall last.

Now!—What's to do with all your time,
And all that money too?
Those great big checks you'll get each month,
Just think—its all for you!

Some clothes?—a trip?—we just don't know,
One hardly can decide.
Or maybe nothing of the kind,
That money you'll just hide.

Now don't you mind what others think,
You stay at home—or go.
Just hide that cash—or spend it all,
It's yours to keep or blow.

There's so much more, that should be said,
About your working life,
Or how besides your working out,
You've been, mother, maid and wife.

You've been the cook that fixed the meals,
You've kept the house intact.
You've taught good manners to the kids,
You've showed them how to act.

You've been a tutor for the boys,
You've taught them right from wrong.
You've been a nursemaid when they're ill,
Would sing to them a song.

You've served the churches where we've been,
Taught class and led "W-M,"
Made pastoral visits, with all this,
To bring the families in.

You've seen the sick, and weary ones,
Helped others where you could.
Stood by your man in trying times,
As Pastor's helpmate should.

We could go on and say much more,
About your busy life.
But space won't let us write all things,
About this "Working Wife."

Yes, you deserve retirement now,
So wipe away the tears;
You've waited long and worked so hard,
Enjoy your "Golden Years."

And now our prayer—
"God grant you health,
In all the years ahead.
May you know peace and happiness,
As by God's hand you're led."

Freddie

8/21/92

SICK AND TIRED

I'm sick and tired
Of being tired and sick,
And no one seems to care.
I push myself
From day to day,
My illness must be rare.

My test all come back
Negative,
No problems can be found.
From EKG's to Echo-gram,
I seem to be quite sound.

But still I hurt
Much weakness feel,
I'm losing weight each week.
As days pass by
I try by best,
An answer I do seek.

My loving wife
God bless her soul,
Can't seem to understand.
She's not real sure
If I'm really sick,
Or just "sympathy" demand.

My doctor thinks
It's in my head,
Just "nerves" I hear him say.
Now try this pill
If it doesn't help,
See me another day.

I've asked the Lord
To meet my need,
But he's not chosen to heal.
Just what's to do
To get some help,
For a problem that is real?

I'll just press on
Each day I'll rise,
Though nauseous and with pain.
And push to do appointments
  set,
In sunshine or in rain.

Perhaps I'm blue—
A little bit,
'Cause no one does believe.
I'm really sick
And need some help,
My misery to relieve.

I've just one hope
And that's in God,
Though as yet he's chosen to wait.
My faith to test
My love to prove,
Or let nature bring my fate.

I'll still believe
What 'ere be tide,
Keep faith, this is a must.
I'll keep on praying
For my health,
In God I'll keep my trust.

08/28/91

SLEEP ON

Sleep on—Sleep on
And take you rest,
While I go out
To face the Quest.

Sleep on—Sleep on
As I go on,
Before the rising
Of the sun.

Sleep on while I
My coffee drink,
And all alone
Just sit and think.

Sleep on as I
A dollar make,
To tide us o'er
'Ere budget break.

Oh, yes—Sleep on
I must be gone,
For day is now
About to dawn.

SLEEPING BEAUTY

Sleep on, my Sleeping Beauty,
I love you much , my little "Cutie."
I must go now and do my duty,
If I expect to make some "Lootie."

(Eight bells and all is well)

02/06/73

SLIM AND TRIM

My dearest Evelyn, trim and
   slim,
Here's just a note for you.
I'm on my way just up the
   street,
To fix a note or two.

Or maybe ten instead of two,
Then pull up all the strings.
And tune it sweet from end
   to end,
Till lovely music rings.

I should be home somewhere
   'round four,
If everything goes well.
But I don't know how bad it is,
It's really hard to tell.

I put some "deer" in roasting pan,
Not smelling very good.
But I just thought it might be nice,
To cook it for my food.

The sausage you can let it thaw,
So patties I can make.
For breakfast in the early morn,
Just from the freezer take.

I must get on and do my stuff,
So I can hurry back.
With jobs all done for me today,
But I haven't made much "jack."

Love,
Freddie

1/17/83

SPRING AND YOU

There's nothing quite refreshing
Like a welcome day of spring.
The beauty of the sunshine
Somehow just make you sing.

The pretty little flowers,
The grass so fresh and green.
The breeze so pure and gentle,
Gives life new hope it seems.

The plowing by the farmers,
The raking of the yard.
The hope of finding mushrooms,
And painting, though it's hard.

Yet even amid the cleaning,
The hoeing and the rest.
Somehow it seems that springtime,
Is the season I like best.

And as I think today of spring,
I think of you my love.
Your presence is as welcome,
As the sunshine from above.

SUMMER'S SLIPPING BY

The summer's here—and
   slipping by,
July is well nigh past.
I've often wondered from a lad,
Just why can't summer last?

As winter days pass slowly by,
I long for spring to come.
Then summer days arrive at last,
Can bask in sun and fun.

Enjoy some sports and visit
   friends,
A cycle trip or two;
Vacation days in Disney World,
Watch evening's sunset hue.

Since just a child I've dreamed
   of days
Vacation never ends.
At least from May till Labor
   Day,
The entire summer spend.

I'd leave my work and worry, too,
Locked up all left behind.
Then I would go with Evelyn
   Dear,
No worry on our mind.

We'd take in sights from north
   to south,
And east to west as well.
We'd see it all along the way,
Just listen, let me tell.

There's Martha's Vineyard in
   the east,
Niagara Falls, I'm sure.
Across the border to the north,
Some other sights would lure.

The Big Grand Canyon in
   the west,
See desert cactus, too.
Then California, Mexico,
The big St. Louis Zoo.

Alaska is a "must" you know,
The Yukon on the way.
Who knows—such beauty oh
   so vast,
May bid our souls to stay.

Hawaii, oceans, east and west,
With all that's in between.
'twould grip our hearts as on
   we go,
Such sights we'd never seen.

continued

But Wait! I must awake to facts.
That's only meant for some.
My time of wishing here must
   end,
For me 'twill never come.

So here I sit, my coffee near,
With pencil in my hand.
I'm at McDonald's restaurant,
Just dreaming—surf and sand.

The summer's here—it's
   slipping by,
July is well nigh past.
I ask again as yesteryear,
"Oh why, can't summer last?"

July 28, 1987

THE GIFT

What shall we give is often asked,
When baby showers come.
A shawl or blanket, pants or dress,
Or diapers - might give some.

When all these thoughts had been explored,
And nothing seemed to click.
A new thought came into my head,
To me seemed pretty slick.

To Little Levi, Joe or Pete,
Or maybe Cheryl Ann.
This gift we give to start you out,
With all the love we can.

The name you see, it will be changed,
When little one is here.
And savings plan will be in force,
To grow from year to year.

With Love,
Grandma and Grandpa Rice

02/21/80

The Morn After Christmas

'Twas the morn after Christmas,
When all through the house,
Not a creature was stirring,
Not even my spouse.

The gifts all were opened,
The house was a mess.
So we'll sleep and forget it,
Was her thought I would guess.

But with Dad it's all different,
Such joys not his lot.
It's go tune pianos,
Whether "zero" or hot.

So, with my coffee all gone,
And my tools in the car.
Its out in the darkness,
Terre Haute seems so far.

But no—I hear something,
A creak in the floor.
She's up now to kiss me,
'Ere I go out the door.

12/21/73

THE TREASURE HUNT

A treasure hunt again this year,
Not quite the same as last.
But 'twill be fun for you my dear,
So start to think…now fast!

What can it be…where is it hid,
In house, in yard or church?
You've got to find that secret lid,
That box or hidden perch.

Now you might go out to the car,
The new Olds you might try.
Just open up the trunk back there,
And neath the spare tire pry.

Not there? How sad! Let's try again,
To the front room you might go.
And by the couch, stoop down and bend,
And look beneath so low.

Not there again, "It just ain't fair,
To do this way," you say.
But patience now, my lady fair,
Will be worth it all some day.

No, I'll not send you to the church,
That might be slightly much.
Nor to the barn, out there to search,
I'd never think of such.

Why don't you think to go upstairs?
Into my room proceed.
Look in my closet…watch for bears,
Of varmints, must take heed.

No, really dear, it's not that bad,
A mess, though, you might find.
But don't you care…and don't get mad,
Just don't you pay no mind.

continued

Go to the end where suits are hung,
And scoot them from the wall.
Now midst that mess…and there among,
Some things should start to fall.

Oh, there it is! Down on the floor,
Behind that pile of stuff.
Now pull it out, some Christmas more,
I hope it is enough.

Now, back downstairs beneath the tree,
Let's open up your gift.
And what's in there you'll get to see,
As from its box you lift.

P.S. I trust my gifts will meet your need,
May they some joy impart.
This is my loving Christmas deed,
I give them from my heart.

Love,
Freddie

Christmas "1975"

THOSE GOLDEN YEARS

You've reached that magic golden age,
You never thought would come.
But years did pass, yes, all too fast,
You've joined that rank with some.

This saga started years ago,
When you were just a child.
A story never ending,
It almost drives one wild.

You first aspired to be thirteen,
This age a milestone.
The next would be to turn sixteen,
Could go on dates alone.

Then twenty-one when you could vote,
That really gave you clout.
But even then, not sure you knew,
What life was all about.

The twenties passed you all to quick,
"Three-O" you did not want.
For years were passing much too fast,
Your youth you could not flaunt.

The thirties now were slipping by,
And forties loomed so big.
You hair got thin about that time,
You had to wear a wig.

Your big "Four-O" was quite a bash,
With friends and family near.
The church, it gave "This is Your Life,"
Your past quite fun to hear.

Those forties—fifties, swiftly flew,
Your boys grown up and gone.
You only—with your man were left,
Both sitting there alone.

continued

Then came retirement—could it be,
You're really growing old?
And headed down that road ahead,
Some people say is Gold?

Next came the age of sixty-two,
With "old age" pension check.
Social security, to be sure,
Does this mean life's a wreck?

The next three years moved all too fast,
As days flew swiftly by.
You tried not to give it too much thought,
Though tempted oft to cry.

But not to worry nor to fret,
Don't go into a rage.
You've Medicare to pay your doc,
This is that "Golden Age."

Yes, now that day has finally come,
Another milestone.
Age "65" it's really here,
A fact you must condone.

There are thousands who have walked that road,
And none the worse for wear.
See happy seniors all around,
Who do not show despair.

So come, let's face those golden years,
And really have some fun.
Things not enjoyed in years gone by,
Because you had no "mon."

Go! Do some things! Some places see
"Live up" your golden years.
And since you know the Lord above,
You'll face them without fears.

With All My Love,
Freddie

8-31-95

Thoughts of Mother

The special day has come again,
To honor Mother dear.
This day is one looked
   forward to,
From year and unto year.

What can we say that's not been
   said,
What shall be this year's theme.
Might speak of love—home—
   patience too,
But songs of these we've seen.

Might tell of kindness—extra
   things,
Might think of food she's
   cooked.
Might ponder on the sacrifice,
As back ore life we look.

Could tell of work, both home
   and out,
And shifts both day and night.
All way from Tarzian to
   Blue Cross,
Some jobs have been a sight.

And all these things were done
   to help,
And keep the needs all met.
So on this day I'd like to pay,
A tribute different yet.

I rack my brain - and try to
   think,
Of words that've not been said.
But try I may, they just don't
   come,
Into my thinking head.

I guess the reason nothing's new,
Is 'cause fellows just like me,
Have tried each year for subjects
   more,
So "Mom" their love could see.

Perhaps there's something more
   than words,
Yes, more than flowers too.
Ah! Here it is, just what I've
   sought,
To show my love to you.

continued

Not just this day, but all year through,
My gratitude I'll show.
By loving deeds and actions kind,
<u>This</u> theme will let you know.

Now Mother Dear with this corsage,
Down payment now I make.
My IOU for days to come,
I trust—in love—you'll take.

Date: May 14, 1967
Indianapolis, IN

PAY TO: THE "MOTHER" OF MY TWO SONS

365 DAYS OF LOVE AND KINDNESS

I.O.U
Payable Day by Day

Three Days Till Christmas

Three days till Christmas
That wonderful day,
When we gather 'round the tree
To pass the presents
Both large and small,
With all wondering..."What's
   for me?"

There'll be some gifts
We'd hoped would come,
And some not expected at all.
There's apt to be some
That will make us laugh,
And others might make us bawl.

This year I'm afraid
My wife has gone,
And bought far more than she
   should.
But I must confess,
I've extended myself,
And have bought all the gifts
   that I could.

The boys are the ones
Who started it all,
With their great big spending
   spree.
Expensive gifts,
For everyone,
Especially for mom and me.

No...no one's guilty,
Yet we all are too,
But only because of LOVE.
And want to reflect
That Heavenly Gift,
That came to the world from
   above.

Each day we say,
"What more can I add
To what is already there?"
So gift by gift
The packages mount,
And I'm sure I'll get more than
   my share.

continued

Now with three days to go,
And money all spent,
And charge accounts to the limit
What more can I get,
What more can I give,
And then I say..."Just wait a minute."

I'll give of myself,
I'll give of my thoughts,
I'll write them a poem, you see.
A gift that is different,
Uniquely from me,
And dollar-wise, it will be FREE.

So, along with the gifts,
Here is my ode,
I trust it will happiness bring.
And on this great day,
As we share in our joy
LET THE BELLS OF CHRISTMAS RING.

12/22/67

P.S. I've written verses
From time to time,
And some have been fairly long.
But this one is longer
Than ever before,
And I know you will say that I'm wrong.

Just fact....no brag,
And this is true,
For I'm writing as I drive.
And at Lafayette
I started all this,
Michigan City's now in sight.

Some ninety miles
This poem is long,
So this, now don't you forget.
A poem that covers
All of those miles,
It <u>must</u> be the longest yet.

To Go or Not to Go

Those famous words ring down through time,
"To be or not to be."
Yes, questions always linger on,
No clear-cut path I see.

A question much like that of old,
I ponder often so,
I ask each day—no answer comes,
"To go or not to go."

I try to weigh the pros and cons,
Of leaving all behind.
To head for sunshine in the south,
Another life to find.

I guess I'm scared, down deep inside,
Such drastic move to make.
To find employment—home—and all
Seems such a chance to take.

The pluses, some are sure to be
Like living in the sun.
We'd sell the house and pay our bills,
I'm sure we'd have some fun.

We'd have some money left in hand,
Invest and feel secure.
We'd have less worry over work,
Less house upkeep I'm sure.

I could go on and tell about
That more relaxing life.
Like fish and boat, enjoy the beach,
Just me and yes—my wife.

On other hand the "cons" are there,
Which one should balance too.
Before decisions as big as that,
Are made to try things new.

Our home we've had for eighteen years,
Has become part of our life.
There are jobs and friends—most everything,
And very little strife.

If both should live, it's wise to stay,
With everything intact.
But if our life were shortened some,
We face another fact.

continued

Then might as well enjoy the sun,
The surf and all the rest.
And take our money left in
   hand,
With it we would invest.

I'm not too sure just how 'twill be,
I'm pondering all this so.
Some day I'll find the answer
   of—
"To go or not to go".

5-9-84
McDonald's – Greenwood

TO MY SLEEPING BEAUTY

The time has come
For me to go.
The work it must be done.

The cement men
Will be there,
By rising of the sun.

It falls my lot
To supervise
This project from the start.

So here I go
This early morn,
For I must do my part.

If I don't fail
But faithful be,
The church will be complete.

Then glad I'll be
That I was there,
To help pour this concrete.

8/28/72

My Tribute to Dad (Cronkhite)

My mind rolls back across the years,
'Twas June of forty-eight.
I met a man with strength and youth,
Full ten is how I'd rate.

I met his wife and daughters four,
Fine family one could see.
Not knowing then in course of time,
My father-in-law he'd be.

It's been my joy to be his son,
To love him through the years.
To share with him and family too,
Their joys and yes, their tears.

Remember Dad - his days of strength,
Hard work was his forte.
Up long 'fore dawn to start his chores,
Then in the field all day.

Six days to labor was his code,
The seventh leave the soil.
And join with others of like faith,
To hear the Word of God.

His Lord came first in everything,
Farm, friends and family too.
Acknowledged God in all His ways,
As Scriptures say to do.

He's known his sorrow through the years,
Five children laid to rest.
But found God's grace in every case,
With strength to stand the test.

'Twas hard to give his parents up,
His sisters gone ahead.
And Dad will know his day will come,
And face it without dread.

One might go on and make a list,
His virtues fill a book.
As back across, plus eighty years,
That we together look.

The years have passed, his days
   are gone,
And tears now fill our eyes.
For time has come for each of us,
To say earth's last "good-byes."

But sorrow now, we have a hope,
This written, Paul has said.
A hope beyond this veil of tears,
He'll rise up from the dead.

Reunion then with those who
   are gone,
With freedom from life's fears.
No pain nor sorrow over there,
God has wiped away his tears.

We would not want to call
   him back,
From Heaven's golden shore.
For blessings sweet, yes joys
   untold,
Are his forevermore.

He can't return, the Psalmist said,
But we can go to be.
With him and those gone on
   before,
For all eternity.

10/23/85
Driving up to the farm for Dad's service.

To My Sweetheart
on Valentine's Day 1965

This little gift
To you I give,
Because I love you so.
It's just a way
That I can use,
To let my Sweetheart know.

The gift is small
As you can see,
That doesn't matter much.
It's what's behind
These little rings,
The sentiment and such.

I trust these rings
Will bring you joy,
And happiness - no end.
It's with that thought
And deep desire,
These rings to you I send.

You are my Love
And Valentine,
And always you will be.
Accept these rings
As tokens true,
And in them my love see.

With love,
Freddie

2/12/65

Weekend With Two Granddaughters in Gatlinburg July 4-6, 1986

A cycle trip I thought to make,
The Smokies I would see.
No, not alone, for I would take,
My wife along with me.

A Grandma true in all her ways,
The thought came 'cross her mind.
Why don't we drive and Amber take,
'Twould be a gesture kind.

In course of days - we were to learn,
That Courtney would be here.
"Let's take them both", heard Grandma say,
That sounded - Oh, so dear.

So cycle trip was set aside,
And plans were made to take
The grandkids down to Gatlinburg,
Yes, just for Grandma's sake.

We'd leave real early Friday morn,
Arrive down there mid-day.
So grips were packed and swimsuits, too.
"We're ready," kids did say.

On Thursday night no one could sleep,
The kids all filled with glee.
So long 'fore midnight, I said "Let's go,"
Grandma agreed with me.

continued

On down the road near Louisville,
The kids both fell asleep.
We drove on through the night till dawn,
They never made a peep.

'Bout nine o'clock we did arrive,
Our room awaiting us.
We checked right in and got unpacked,
Without a bit of fuss.

First on the list, we'd check the pools,
Found three and sauna, too.
A wading pool and holidome,
So much it seemed untrue.

From there we took a walk downtown,
Took chair-lift up the mount.
Then here and there, did this and that
Too much to try and count.

That haunted house, we'll ne'er forget,
The kids just had to go.
Before we found the exit door,
They both were crying "No."

Back to the pools to swim a bit,
And rest our weary feet.
For soon we had to go again,
And find some food to eat.

A night of rest we needed BAD,
Before another day.
By morning light, the kids were up,
Quite chipper, pert and gay.

'Twas Dollywood we headed for,
When breakfast was complete.
To fight the traffic and the crowd,
We found it quite a feat.

To name the things we did that day,
Would be too big a job.
By shortly after noon, we said,
"Let's go and beat the mob."

Back to the room and welcome pool,
We found a fine retreat.
The kids could swim while grandma sat
Again to rest her feet.

We headed home on Sunday morn,
Would stop that very day.
Let Amber see her Grandpa Kries,
As it was on the way.

Had been some time since he had seen
This little girl, age six.
By now she's nine and grown a lot,
And learned a few new tricks.

From Knoxville then we headed north,
The girls sat in the back.
Amused themselves all the way,
With games of this and that.

They never slept or even
   hushed,
For all those many miles.
They kept the old folks up in
   front,
With chuckles, laughs and
   smiles.

We made it home all safe and
   sound,
Without a single hitch.
That cycle trip for these few
   days,
We'd never want to switch.

WORK DAY

Here my boys is a very good way,
To spend your time and pass your day.
These things I'm expecting to be done,
Before the setting of the sun.

1. Some clothes you'll find in basket fair.
   Hang up to dry and get fresh air.

2. The grass is long, it must be cut,
   Lower the wheels and tighten the nut.

3. By now you might be out of puff,
   so rest awhile, you've done enough.

4. The house, it must be cleaned up now,
   read very close, I'll tell you how.

5. The downstairs isn't very bad,
   just straighten it for your old Dad.

6. Upstairs the dirt's a litter deeper,
   I think you better run the sweeper.

7. The bathroom, it is worse yet,
   Ajax is needed I will bet.

8. Again you've worked now quite a bit,
   I think you better stop and sit.

9. By now the house should look quite nice,
   don't be too tough when you set the price.

10. Clean you up now, hands, ears and nose,
    and put you on some cleaner clothes.

11. By two, I'll be home to fix our lunch,
    We'll all sit down and munch and crunch.

12. I'll take you to the Tribune-Star,
    Then you can tell them who you are.

13. Walk home real slow and
    don't you run,
    you'll get too sweaty in the
    sun.

14. Mom wants you to be
    cleaned up good,
    so you can go with her to
    get some food.

15. And with this my poem will
    end,
    I'm proud of you my little
    men.

Love,
Dad

July 26, 1963

The dishes, I forgot to mention,
I see them stacked up in the
    kitchen
So since it's me that made the
    goof,
I'll do them for you - good
    enough?

WORKDAY

I did cooking.
I did washing.
I did ironing,
All this morning.

Did the dishes,
Hung the clothes out.
Burnt the trash,
And rubbed the dog's snout.

Got some money,
For my honey.
Wrote the check,
For eight bucks only.

Did some shopping,
Without stopping.
Made a tape,
Man, I've been hopping.

Time is running,
Boys are coming.
Start in fixing,
Food or something.

Rush is over,
All is still now.
I'm all in,
But must go anyhow.

See you later,
Alligator,
Hope you're pleased,
My little 'mater.

05/25/64
(Mo wrote, "My Sweetie, wrote this,
I love him".)

The Rice Reunion

The years have come,
The years have gone,
Since our reunion started.
As we look back
Across the years,
So many have departed.

The families that
Made up this clan,
Date back, three Rice brothers.
There's William, Harvey,
Whitten, too,
Don't know of any others.

The family tree,
It grew and grew,
We loved each other dear.
So someone said,
Let's make our plans
To meet each coming year.

As I recall,
There's William's clan,
With Harvey, Mable Sweet.
And with their family
Used to come,
Their loved ones all to meet.

Then Harvey's clan,
With Dan and Bill,
Fate, Paul and all the rest.
Aunt Flora came
And gave a speech,
She really was the best!

From Whitten's clan
Were Fred and Jim,
There were Ida and Aunt Mae.
It's hard to name
Just everyone,
But they all led the way.

(Hope to finish some time...)

Editor's Note

Fred went home to be with the Lord on October 3, 1996.
Perhaps he's finishing it now . . .

CANDID MUSINGS and PRACTICAL PARABLES

TRIBUTE

A Tribute to my Dad

Whatsoever things are true, whatsoever things are honest, whatsoever things are just, whatsoever things are pure, whatsoever things are lovely, whatsoever things are of good report; If there be any virtue and if there be any praise, think on these things.
Philippians 4:8

My father practiced the above scripture. I think of my dad as the greatest man to ever live. He was a compassionate, humble and gentle man. His entire life was one of service to God, his church, his family and all he met. He was diligent in the carrying out of his responsibilities and he was steadfast in his love for God. He was always there with us during trying times as well as good times.

My dad was a gift from God to all that knew him. God had given him many talents that he used unselfishly for the uplifting of others. He was a man of sacrifice, forsaking monetary gain in order to do what he felt God had called him to do.

His love for his church and his family was only surpassed by his love for God and the things of God. He was a teacher who taught me about life and to put God first in everything I did. His teaching was not merely with words for he would often say, "Actions speak louder than words," but he lived the life he taught.

I love him with all of my heart. He will never be out of my thoughts. I think of him always and I miss him greatly.

Levi M. Rice

MEMORIES OF DAD

How could I ever hope to put into words the feelings I have when I think of my dad? When I consider the many qualities of his life, the unending love, the gentleness, the completeness in his Christian life and walk, I truly marvel.

If one word ever fit my dad's life it would be "pure." His had truly a pure heart and a pure love for everyone! Jesus said in John 13:35, "By this shall all men know that you are my disciples, that you have love one for another." My dad was the most loving man I ever knew. He just gave and gave and gave some more.

Because of his great love for the Lord, and his desire to serve Him, he accepted pastoral positions in many small churches that could not financially support him. He would find second jobs, often manual labor, to feed his small family so that come Sunday he could be in the pulpit preaching the Gospel of Jesus Christ. He would preach of God's endless grace and mercy that reaches down to each one of us.

Dad was a man who knew and understood hard work all his life. He was forced from school at an early age through circumstances of life to find full-time work to help support his parents and siblings. And, he did it all to the glory of God. The Holy Spirit dwelled within him, worked and spoke through him. Because he was filled with the Spirit, his life was a testimony and example to all with whom he came in contact. He was able to draw many people into the saving grace of Jesus Christ through the blameless life that he led and the unending witness that he gave everyday of his life.

It is difficult to convey to people today what constituted "sin" to an Assembly of God preacher in the heart of the Bible Belt in Southern Indiana in the 1950s. Dad used to say, "It's not always what you do or don't do that's right or wrong, but often it's your motive that is the question." As the preacher's kids, it all came down to the example we were presenting to others. Therefore, a strict set of rules had to be in place so that our lives would become examples to others. But to us P.K.'s these strict rules were totally in line. As Po and I would talk in later years about how extreme some of those rules seemed to us now, I would look back at the slingshot effect my life took when I married young and outside the faith, moved away from home and began to experience the pitfalls and traps Satan had laid for me in my life, and I would thank God for every conservative thought my dad ever had. I realize now more than ever that it is only through the grace of God and the prayers of my father that I am alive today. What a comfort and blessing it was to have him for my dad.

Dad's poem, "Keep Faith" written December 16, 1980 to my grieving mother, shows the type of constant comfort he was. Though his heart was heavy, he could still rise above it, with God's help, and be a blessing and comfort to others. His support of me during those years will live with me always.

My dad, the best example of a Christian I have ever known.

Po, I'll always love you,
Freddie

CANDID MUSINGS and PRACTICAL PARABLES

FAMILY ALBUM

Levi, Evelyn, Freddie and Fred

Levi, Fred and Freddie